SKETCHES *of* SPAIN

❖ ❖ ❖ ❖ ❖

Federico García Lorca was born in 1898 in Fuente Vaqueros, a small town near Granada. He studied law and literature at Granada University, during which time he published *Impresiones y paisajes*, and in 1919 moved to Madrid, where he enrolled at the Residencia de Estudiantes and formed friendships with, amongst others, Luis Buñuel, Salvador Dalí and Manuel de Falla. *Libro de Poemas*, his first book of verse, was published in 1921, while his first play, *The Butterfly's Evil Spell*, was performed in Madrid in 1920. His second play, *Mariana Pineda*, with set designs by Dalí, was premièred in Barcelona in 1927 and the following year *Romancero Gitano* (*Gypsy Ballads*) was greeted with great acclaim.

In 1929 Lorca travelled to New York, where, as well as studying at Columbia University, he witnessed the Wall Street Crash, and then to Cuba, where he gave a short series of lectures. The military dictatorship of Primo de Rivera was overthrown in 1930 and when Spain became a republic in 1931 Lorca dedicated himself to the theatre, becoming the artistic director of La Barraca (The Barn), a government-sponsored company that brought some of the great works of Spanish theatre to towns and cities where such plays had never been staged before. During the time he worked with La Barraca, Lorca wrote some of his most widely admired plays, including *Yerma* and *Bodas de Sangre* (*Blood Wedding*).

Clearly identified as a supporter of the Republic, Lorca was abducted and murdered by Francoist insurgents in August 1936, shortly after the outbreak of the Spanish Civil War.

Peter Bush's translations from Spanish, Catalan and Portuguese include work by Juan Goytisolo, Josep Pla, Juan Carlos Onetti and Pedro Almodóvar. He lives in Barcelona.

Julian Bell is a painter and writer whose books include *Mirror of the World: A New History of Art* and *What is Painting? Representation and Modern Art*. He is a regular contributor to the *Guardian* and *London Review of Books*.

SKETCHES *of* SPAIN

✤ ✤ ✤ ✤ ✤ ✤ ✤

Federico García Lorca

translated from the Spanish by Peter Bush

with illustrations by Julian Bell

Serif
London

First published 2013 by
Serif
47 Strahan Road
London E3 5DA

www.serifbooks.co.uk

1 3 5 7 9 8 6 4 2

Originally published as *Impresiones y paisajes* in 1918 by
P.V. Traveset, Granada

Translation, Foreword and Glossary copyright © Peter Bush, 2013
Illustrations copyright © Julian Bell, 2013
This edition copyright © Serif, 2013

British Library Cataloguing in Publication Data.
A catalogue record for this book is available from the British Library.

ISBN 978 1897959 62 6

Designed and set in 9.5 pt Iowan by sue@lambledesign.demon.co.uk

Printed and bound in Great Britain by
TJ International Ltd, Padstow, Cornwall

CONTENTS

❖ ❖ ❖ ❖ ❖

ILLUSTRATIONS BY JULIAN BELL

✣ ✣ ✣ ✣ ✣

FOREWORD

✦ ✦ ✦ ✦ ✦

In 1916 and 1917 Federico García Lorca went on four field trips led by his literature professor at Granada University, Martín Domínguez Berrueta. Lorca, his fellow students and Berrueta travelled extensively in central and north-west Spain, as well as making one trip around Andalusia, where they visited Baeza, Córdoba and Ronda. Berrueta planned the trips so that his students would visit key sites in the history of Spanish culture, study their art and architecture and then write up their experiences. At the same time, these trips were intended to be two-way cultural exchanges. Teacher and students gave public talks, Lorca played the piano and they conversed with local artists, intellectuals and clergy; in Baeza, for example, this meant listening to a recitation by the renowned poet Antonio Machado. Lorca's letters and telegrams to his family are full of cheerful news and enthusiasm for the new sights and sounds he was encountering as well as constant pleas for his father to send more pesetas. In April 1918, aged just nineteen, Lorca published a selection of his writing from those trips, his first book-length publication and his only book of prose: *Impresiones y paisajes* (Impressions and Landscapes).

While his contemporaries in most other European countries were dragooned into the horror of the First World War, in neutral Spain the young Lorca recorded his passionate responses to his country's life and tradition as he found them inscribed in Castile's often fortress-like monasteries and churches on 'emotional walks through warrior Spain'. The decaying buildings, poverty and mystical aura and landscapes had already been the subject of the previous generation of writers. The so-called 1898 generation had split between those, including Antonio Machado, who pilloried 'a Castile that scorns what it doesn't know' and others, like Miguel de Unamuno, who, with his disdainful cry 'Let them invent!', ended up worshipping a Spain that was a redoubt of spirituality in a Europe dominated by science, technology and materialism.

Twenty years later, Lorca had been murdered by fascist insurgents, Unamuno had been forced to step down as rector of Salamanca University after his confrontation with the Francoist General Millán Astray, who bellowed 'Death to Intelligence!', and Machado, like countless other Republicans, had died in exile in France.

Lorca's youthful writing wrestles with the awe inspired by the melancholy beauty of the red plains of Castile, the crumbling grandeur of its ecclesiastical architecture and the horror of poverty. For the modern reader, the retrospective poignancy is no more deeply felt than in his account of the visit to the monastery in San Pedro de Cardeña near Burgos.

The Cid and his wife rest in a tomb 'where their statues lie damaged and soulless [in a] large, ugly church' next to 'a dusty, rubbish-filled cloister' and 'the rest is a ruin, where silvery slugs thread across nettles'. In the Civil War this shrine to the medieval mercenary and hero, beloved by everyone from Victor Hugo to Hollywood, became a sinister hospital in a concentration camp where Gestapo doctors helped Franco's favourite psychiatrist, Antonio Vallejo Nájera, with his tests and experiments on International Brigade prisoners of war in an attempt to identify 'the red gene'.

While Lorca treads what had become well-worn literary paths in the heart of the 'Carthusian austerity' and 'tedious homogeneity' of Castile that so fascinated the Romantics, his is a lyrical prose that already has the unmistakable personal note of the poet who felt sympathy for the poor and was struggling to find his own way as a young homosexual in a profoundly bigoted society, constantly reflecting on the relationship between artist, audience and history. His visit to the tombs in Burgos leads him to reflect on the central role of embellishment in works of art. For Lorca, the medieval artists who carved choir stalls and misericords were elaborating 'sardonically packaged ideas of life and death', things they couldn't say for 'fear of being burnt alive or shut up forever in a dingy prison'. These were 'ordinary folk' lashing out with 'all the rage and perversity they could muster against those who enslaved them'.

On the other hand, in the essay on the Christs he encounters on his travels, he spells out their brutal physicality, the recreation of the 'bruised and battered body in all its spine-chilling reality' by artists wanting to speak to the illiterate populace and stun them into submission and fear. It is as if he is grappling, through his own descriptions of this art that speaks to a contemporary audience, with what it is to be an artist, and with what kind of artist he is and is going to be. He is scathing in his criticism of the blandness of the modern religious art he sees and of modern sculpture like the statue that is a 'hateful gob of spit' on the magnificent façades in Santiago de Compostela's central square.

Lorca's landscapes and impressions are not blind to suffering in the present. He rails against the medieval church but also against what he sees as the false havens of peace from sexual temptation and strife that the monks and nuns he meets have entered in an attempt to escape their passions. He surmises that the cells and cloisters only breed morbid introspection and a life-negating obsession with what drove them there in the first place. This is about sex and other pleasures of the senses. As a musician, Lorca is entranced by the beauties of the Gregorian plainchant he hears in Santo Domingo de Silos, but is equally horrified by his exchange with an organist there who has never heard Beethoven or the monk, visited by Zuloaga and Unamuno, who abandoned classical music because it was too sensual and tempting. The monk can't bear to hear the brief interlude from the Seventh Symphony that the young writer plays on the organ.

Lorca also draws, in the style of Verlaine and Juan Ramón Jiménez, on the eighteenth-century, Watteauesque melancholy of gardens, yet punctures it with wry humour at his own expense. In the Gardens suite he decries the invasion of 'tidy, symmetrical English parks', lamenting that, 'The madrigal died with the birth of the railway.' However the young man visiting the garden seems to acquiesce before the poor mother and her children eking out a living from the vegetables they produce on the allotment they are cultivating in the Marchioness's arbour. His most bitter-sweet sarcasm is reserved for the station-garden roses struggling to survive a diet of alcoholic leftovers, coffee grouts, coal dust and soot.

If Castile is a tragic rhapsody, Lorca's Granada erupts in a symphony of life, colour, birds and bells, with the occasional grotesque scherzo, in the shadow of the Alhambra, the palace of the Nasrid kings until 1492. The days are splendidly light, the towers graceful, the city magnificent. The Albaicín is full of reminders of the Arab past and a fatalism that is salvaged by golden hills and 'the bustle and bite of flamenco'. Nightmarish visions of filth and prostitution give way to the sonorous landscape from the Alhambra to the Sierra Nevada and the 'magnificent counterpoint' to the cathedral bells' tenor key from the belfries of the Albaicín, whose tones suggest the lives of the ringers: the playful novice, grumpy old sacristan and a nun 'awaiting the scythe's cut'. Andalusia sparks a lyricism that is never darkened by the morbid oppression Lorca found in Castile.

On these journeys and in this early prose the poet was deciding to abandon what had until then seemed to be his chosen profession as a musician. It is a prose full of music in its sound and themes. The ecstatic evocations of light and colour in Andalusia, together with the intricate and meticulous description of nature, foreshadow the poems in his first volume of verse, *Libro de poemas*, which was to be published three years later. Lorca himself never stopped travelling – to New York and Cuba, later to Argentina – and during the Republic would return to the road and Spain's remote towns and villages with the travelling theatre troupe, La Barraca.

Critics have noted that Lorca's first book was full of spelling and punctuation oddities, how he was driven by the flow of his words, tending not to worry about 'the normative aspect of language'. In this translation, I have tried to recreate the rich, rhapsodic yet self-reflective flow that reflects Lorca's originality at such a young age. Julian Bell's remarkable drawings are the perfect visual accompaniment to Lorca's architecture in prose.

I would like to dedicate this translation to Geoffrey Parkinson, my Spanish teacher, who, fifty years ago, led a few enthusiasts to read the whole of Lorca's poetry at the age of eighteen.

Peter Bush

Barcelona
August 2012

To the respected memory of my old music teacher whose gnarled hands so often pulsated on the piano and inscribed rhythms on the air, hands he ran through his twilight silvery hair like a smitten gallant suffering ancient passions invoked by a Beethoven sonata. A saint!

With my deeply felt devotion.

The author

alley in the Albaicín, Granada

PROLOGUE

❖ ❖ ❖ ❖ ❖

Friend and reader: if you read the whole of this book, you will recognise a rather vague melancholy. You will see things that fade and pass on, and things portrayed always bitterly, if not sadly. The scenes parading through its pages are interpretations of memories, landscapes and people. Perhaps reality doesn't lift its snow-white head, but, consumed by inner states of passion, fantasy spills its spiritual fire over external nature, magnifying the small and granting dignity to ugliness, like a full moon when it floods the open fields. Something inhabits our soul that surpasses everything that exists. A something that usually slumbers, but, when we remember or find ourselves pleasantly far away, it stirs and embraces scenes it makes part of our personality. That is why we all see things differently. Our feelings soar above the souls of colour and music, but awake in almost no one to spread their wings and embrace such wondrousness. Poetry exists everywhere, in the ugly, the beautiful and the loathsome; what is simply difficult is finding the means to seek it out and stir the deep lagoons of the soul. What is admirable about the spirit is its ability to receive an emotion and interpret it in so many different, contrary ways. And travel the world so that, when we reach the gateway to the 'solitary road', we can drain our cup of all existing emotions, virtue, sin, purity and darkness. In order to interpret, we must always pour our soul over things, see the spiritual where it doesn't exist, and endow forms with the magical *frisson* we feel. We must catch a glimpse of the ancient souls who once walked the solitary squares we now tread; it is essential to be one and a thousand, to experience things in their myriad shades. We must be religious and profane, combine the mysticism of an austere Gothic cathedral with the wonder of pagan Greece. See everything, feel everything. In eternity we will be rewarded for never abiding by set horizons. Love and charity towards everyone, respect for everyone, will lead us into the kingdom of the ideal. We must dream. Wretched the man who doesn't, because he shall never see the light ... This poor book reaches your hands, reader and friend, full of humility. You laugh, don't like this, read only the prologue, you mock ... no matter, nothing lost, nothing gained ... it is one more bloom planted in the impoverished garden of provincial literature ... A few days in the shop windows and then it will be cast into the sea of indifference. If you read and enjoy it, that is also of no matter. I will simply feel an exquisite, much appreciated sense of gratitude ... I say that sincerely. Now take a walk through these pages.

✦ ✦ ✦ ✦ ✦

The curtain rises. The soul of the book is ready to be judged. The reader's eyes are two genii seeking flowers of the spirit to embellish thought. Every book is a garden. Lucky the man who can plant it out and blessed the man who cuts its roses and feeds his soul! The lamps of fantasy light up when they scent the perfumed balm of emotion.

The curtain rises.

MEDITATION

❖ ❖ ❖ ❖ ❖

There is restlessness and death in these silent, forgotten cities. A sound of tolling bells closes around their melancholy ... Distances are short, yet how they exhaust the heart. In some cities, like Ávila, Zamora and Palencia, the air seems iron-clad and the sun spreads infinite sadness over their mysteries and shadows. A loving hand draped itself over their houses to fend off the surge of youthfulness, but the young came and will keep coming, and we shall see an aeroplane soar over the ruddy crosses.

There are souls that suffer from what has been and gone ... and, when they are in ancient mildewed lands imbued with ancestral tranquillity, they forget who they are and contemplate what will never be and, if in turn they look into the future, they cry, sadly, bitterly disillusioned ... These people who walk the deserted streets do so enormously wearied by the deafening red rhythm all around ... The fields!

These fields are an immense symphony of congealed blood without trees, cool respite or shelter for the brain, full of superstitious prayer, broken lances, enigmatic villages, withered men, pitiful offspring of a giant race and august, cruel darkness ... Everywhere there is anguish and aridity, poverty and power ... and fields, yet more fields, all red, all kneaded in the blood of Cain and Abel ... The red cities are almost invisible amid these fields. Cities full of melancholy charm, of memories of tragic loves, of the lives of queens perpetually waiting for a husband who, cross on chest, has gone to war, memories of funeral processions where, afraid of flaming brands, people watched the ravaged faces of holy martyrs fleeing Moorish profanation on their way to be buried, memories of prancing stallions and grim shadows of hanged men, of monkish miracles, of white apparitions in sorrowful prayer leaving belfries when it struck twelve, scattering owls, beseeching the living to take mercy on their souls, memories of the voices of cruel monarchs and the chilling responses of the Inquisition as some heretical astrologer's burnt flesh crackled. The whole of Spain's past and almost its entire present is palpable in the solemnly august cities of Castile ... All the horrors of the Middle Ages, its ignorance and its crimes ... 'The Inquisition was here,' they tell us as we walk by. 'That was the palace of the bishop who organised the *autos de fe*,' then cry, as if seeking a modicum of balance, 'Teresa was born here, Saint John of the Cross there ...'

Cities of Castile full of sanctity, horror and superstition! Cities ruined by progress and now mutilated by civilisation! You are so majestic in your old age, one might almost think there must be a giant soul somewhere, a phantom El Cid shoring up your stones, helping you confront the savage dragons of destruction ... Eras, now blurred and hazy, that passed through your mystical squares. Towering individuals who gave you faith, legends and massive poetry, you still stand, even if threatened by time ... What will future generations tell you? How will the sublime dawn of the future greet you?

Eternal death will lock you into the gentle, honeyed sound of your rivers, and hues of tawny gold will always kiss you when the fiery sun beats down ... You grant the sweetest consolation to romantic souls that our century scorns, you are so romantic, so bygone, and they find tranquillity and blissful exhaustion beneath your carved ceilings ... and the souls wandering your narrow streets, and you, who are so Christian, incite them to pray ... broken crosses in out-of-the-way places or ancient Byzantine saints, cold, stiff and strangely garbed, turtle doves perched on their hands, golden keys or smoky monstrances, set in the tearful porticos of Romanesque churches or in crumbling colonnades ... Dead cities of Castile, an air of immense grief and sorrow hangs over every little thing!

The travelling spirit who passes through your walls, but never contemplates you, is ignorant of the infinite philosophical grandeur you enshrine, and those who live beneath your mantle almost never understand your wondrous gifts of consolation and resignation. A wearied heart satiated by vices and love finds the bitter tranquillity it craves and your incomparably silent nights soothe the spirit that goes in search of you and rages in order to rest and meditate ...

Cities of Castile, you are full of a mysticism that is so

strong and sincere you still the soul! Cities of Castile, when we contemplate your severity, Handel comes to our lips!

✦ ✦ ✦ ✦ ✦

On such emotional walks through warrior Spain, full of awe, the soul and senses enjoy every moment, intoxicated by new feelings that can only be learned here, and when they die they bequeath a magnificent array of memories … To remember a journey is to journey anew, but with more melancholy and a more intense sense of the spell of things … When we remember, we are filled with a sad, gentle light, and our thoughts soar high above all else … We remember streets impregnated with melancholy, people we met, an emotion that swept through us, and we sigh at everything, the streets, the season when we saw them … because, in a word, we re-live the same experience. But if by some trick of Nature we could re-live it again, we wouldn't feel the spiritual pleasure as when our fantasy re-creates … Sweet memories of golden twilights with poplars made of coral, shepherds and flocks huddling next to a hillock, birds swooping across a savage, stifling landscape … Tempered by an exuberant, rebellious imagination, these memories leave a pleasantly sweet aftertaste, and if someone on our travels did us wrong, we forgive them and simply feel scornful pity for ourselves, because we harboured hatred in our hearts; and we understand that the moment is all, and when with a generous heart we look at the world, we cannot but weep … and remember … The red terrain, the sun like the glebe

... farmhands walking along paths hugging close to their animals ... some golden dreamers looking at their solitary reflections in the mellow water of an irrigation channel ... a town-crier ... the distant Angelus ... Castile! We think thus and leaden melancholy burdens our soul.

Plaza de Mosén Rubí, Ávila

ÁVILA

✤ ✤ ✤ ✤ ✤

I arrived on a cold night. There were few stars and a wind slowly glossed the infinite melody of night ... Nobody can speak or tread loudly, or the sublime Teresa's spirit will be frightened away ... You can only feel puny in this mighty city ...

When you pass through its evocative walls you must become religious and live the atmosphere you breathe.

Crowned by storks' nests, these solitary towers seem straight out of a children's fairy story. At any moment you expect to hear a magic horn and see a golden Pegasus ride through the storm clouds over the city and a captive princess make her escape mounted on its back, or to gaze at a band of knights with cloaks and plumes prowling the battlements, brandishing their lances.

The river is scarcely a trickle between the rocky crags, refreshing some stunted trees that cast their shadows over a Romanesque chapel, reliquary of a white sepulchre where a cold bishop prays eternally, hidden among the shadows ... The sun brings deep tranquillity to the golden hills circling the city, and with no trees to offer shade the light burns a magnificent, monotonous red ... Ávila is the most Castilian, most august city on the vast *meseta** ... You never hear strident noises, only a wind that brings violence to its crossroads on winter nights ... Its streets are narrow and most are freezing cold. The houses are grimy with rusty coats of arms, the doors have enormous keystones and are studded with golden nails ... Monuments of great architectural simplicity: severe, massive columns, ingenuous medallions, squat, silent doors and capitals with crude heads and kissing pelicans. And on all sides, crosses with broken staves, knights of old buried in walls and delightful, damp cloisters ... Everywhere the shades of defunct grandeur! The spirit of long, long ago stirs in certain dark squares, and to enter there is to immerse oneself in the fifteenth century. These squares comprise two or three big houses, roofs full of yellow flowers and a single, long balcony. The doorways are closed or in darkness, with an armless saint in a niche and, in the background, light from the countryside slips across a timorous crossroads or a gate in the fortified wall. In the centre a battered cross on a ruined pedestal and suitably ragamuffin children. All under a greyish sky and in a silence in which the river's waters crash like constantly clashing swords.

✤ ✤ ✤ ✤ ✤

---

* The *meseta* is the high tableland of central Spain, home to Ávila, Burgos, Santo Domingo de Silos and other places described by Lorca in this book.

walls of Ávila

An imposing blood-black cathedral, epic brainchild of Bishop Tostado, drips honey from its towers and the bells fill it with an ideal religiosity … The shadows from the past embedded in the temple's walls create an oppressive interior and the tranquil darkness invites meditation on what is supreme.

May the soul of the believer, full of faith in heaven, dream in this cathedral raised by iron kings from a warrior age. May the soul that sees the greatness of Jesus plunge into these humid, candle-eyed shadows and feel spiritual consolation … In some corner listening to the magical organ and a small bell solemnly tinkling, it can think, be unseen and enjoy a

Lane behind the Cathedral, Ávila

sweetness found only there. That is true adoration of God, and is never accompanied by lights, trumpets and a lurid statue resting ridiculously on a bed of rag flowers ... This cathedral gives food for thought even if the soul walking along its galleries doesn't possess the light of faith ... This cathedral is a reflection from the beyond rooted in an interrogation of the past ... Incense and wax create a marmoreal, mystical air to soothe the senses ... Some places harbour forgotten sepulchres with mutilated statues and paintings that are indefinite blotches where a frightened face or naked leg occasionally peers out enigmatically. Many of the high windows are slanted and closed to the light, and their images are silhouetted on the wall. Silver lamps stamp their yellowing souls on the sacred shadows, and a large crucifix poised above the crossing-point adds a layer of sacred whiteness to the apse's ashen light ... Old women with long, heavy rosaries sigh and mouth syllables next to the stoups and one ugly creature prays and whimpers to a Virgin with a silvery heart on her breast and a ridiculous fawn at her feet. The sound of distant footsteps, followed by solitary anguished sounds, fills the soul with bitter sweetness ... When we leave the cathedral, the reredos in the entrance glows in the afternoon sun that turns its tracery and the holy apostles golden, and two scaly monsters with human faces remind passers-by of the ancient, generous right of refuge ... Along streets gilded by the calm of twilight we emerge onto a square with a golden church the evening is transforming into a huge topaz ... And from an ancient wall we contemplate solitary fields in the prelude to night. Over the hills and towards the horizon, a ruddy glow, and over the fields, pale yellow pollen. The city is orange-tinged and the bells peal for the Angelus in the dreamy, balmy air ... Night descends slowly, pine trees sway gracefully in the shadows and storks from the city walls fly over a belfry ... The moon will soon transmute gold into silver.

A TAVERN IN CASTILE

❖ ❖ ❖ ❖ ❖

I saw a tavern on a golden hill next to the silvery river of the road.

Bored by the years that have gone by, the sprawling building infused the huge Romanesque faith of these auburn hues with melancholy.

In these old taverns where surly men lurk under cloaks, breathless and averting their gaze, the might of a dead Spanish spirit lives on ... The one I saw could well have been a background for a character painted by José de Ribera, El Españoleto.

Snotty-nosed kids, the kind always covered in crumbs and clutching a piece of bread, were skulking in the doorway by an ochre-painted, cracked stone bench and an arrogant sultan rooster, his iridescent plumes luring randy hens with playful, flirtatious necks.

The fields were so huge and the song of the land so majestic that the big old house sank its puny rump into the belly of the remote horizon ... The wind thudded in the eardrums like the bow of a giant double-bass; hens clucked and children shouted to high heaven while fighting over a glass marble …

It was like entering a hovel. The grimy walls were sticky with grease and yellowy black encrusted crevices where spiders shone their silken stars.

The pantry was in one corner, littered with uncorked bottles, a broken bowl, tin plates battered by long use, and two big barrels, the kind that reek of wine that is too bad to be true.

It was like a wooden recess smeared with blackish lard where thousands of flies had taken up residence.

When the breeze and the children quietened down, all you could hear was the nervous whir of insect wings and the snorting of mules in the stable next-door.

Then, a heavy, rich smell of sweat and dung began to stifle everything.

On the ceiling, thick, fly-decked ropes perhaps marked the place where someone had hanged himself; a sleepy lad rudely stretched out his arms at midday, a disgusting fag-end between his Egyptian lips; a sunburnt, fair-haired kid played; a bumble-bee buzzed; old men lay like sacks on the ground and snored, their worn-out hats over their faces; in hellish stables gang-masters made little bells jingle as they harnessed their mounts, while behind them, among the shadows at the back of the house, the purest jewel of a stove gave the gawping serving-girl the dull shine of enamelled Limoges copper.

Everyone was dozing in the silent, fly-ridden, airless calm, in the midst of abject poverty.

An old clock, the type that stutters when announcing the time, struck a rancid, solemn twelve o'clock. A blue-smocked charcoal burner came in scratching his head and, whispering unintelligibly, greeted the innkeeper, an ugly, pregnant woman with dishevelled hair and bags under her eyes …

'Want a glass?'

'No,' he said, 'I got a sore throat.'

'You just come from the village?'

'No, I've just been to see my sister, who got that new sickness …'

'If she was rich,' answered the ugly woman, 'the doctor'd have cured her by now … Y' know … the poor …' And the man gestured wearily, repeating, 'The poor …! The poor …!' And as they moved closer, they mumbled on about the same old story of the poverty-stricken.

Then, woken by their noisy conversation, the others started chatting, because nothing makes people talk more than sitting under the same roof with complete strangers … and they all cheered up except for the pregnant woman, whose eyes and movements bore the weary air of one who sees death or feels it is nigh.

That woman was undoubtedly the most interesting person in the inn.

Soon it was time to eat and they all took greasy paper and leather-black bread from their bags, put them on the dusty floor, opened their knives and began their daily task.

They picked up their meagre food in their stony mitts, lifted them to their mouths with religious unction and then wiped them on their trousers.

The innkeeper poured red wine into filthy glasses; clouds of flies flew over the sweetish jars, fell in pairs on the crocks and were rescued from death by the owner's gnarled fingers.

Stifling aromas of bacon, stables and sunny fields wafted in.

In one corner, between sacks and planks, the young lad who had been stretching his limbs gulped down the lurid soup the serving-girl brought him and, to much laughter, attempted activities that were not entirely becoming.

The wine and food enlivened the travellers and, happier or sadder than the rest, the odd one hummed a monotonous ditty.

And one o'clock struck, and half-past one, and two, and nothing changed.

The peasant figures continued to file past, all seemingly alike, their eyes always half-closed from the habit of seeing the whole of life in the fields and under the sun ... and those women walked by, gnarled limbs, sickly eyes and hunched backs, moving pitifully on, seeking a cure in the neighbouring city; thousands of traders filed through, whips in their sashes, men who are tall and loud-mouthed in the tavern, and those Castilians, who are naturally slaves, subdued and polite, still living in fear of their feudal lord and master, always answering, '*Señor! Señor!*' when spoken to ... and men from other regions, who emphasise their words to attract attention ... and a conjurer even dropped in on that picturesque scene, one who goes from village to village, extracting ribbons from mouths and changing the colour of roses ... And two, and half-past two, struck and nothing changed... As there was now some shade in the entrance, they all went out to enjoy the perfumed breeze from the hills ...

Only two old men, on their last legs, stayed dozing inside, fly-blown, their half-open shirts revealing a tuft of grey hair on their chests, as if to underline the demise of their youthful vigour.

Outside you could breathe in the famous breeze from the hillsides that carried in its soul the sweet secret of those scents.

The soft, dry herbs on cool, gently sloping hills were an invitation to climb their table-flat tops.

Massive white clouds coasted over the distant sierras.

A cart approached along the track yoked with oxen, walking so slowly, blinking huge opal blue eyes, gently voluptuous, slavering as if chewing the tastiest morsel ... And more down-at-heel carts passed by, the carters crouching down and sad donkeys, bored out of their minds, loaded down with bracken, goaded by young kids, and men, men we shall never see again, who lead their own lives and are suspicious of anyone who looks askance ... and august silences redolent with sound and colour ...

Three o'clock struck ... and four ...

The afternoon slipped by, honeyed and wondrous ...

✦ ✦ ✦ ✦ ✦

The sky began to compose its symphony in the lower key of twilight. The orangey sky opened out its royal robes. Shoots of melancholy sprang from the distant pines, opening hearts to the infinite music of the Angelus …

The golden earth is blinding. Far-off places dream of nightfall.

LA CARTUJA

✤ ✤ ✤ ✤ ✤

For he that soweth to his flesh shall of the flesh reap corruption; but he that soweth to the Spirit shall of the Spirit reap life everlasting.

The Epistle of Paul the Apostle to the Galatians, VI, 8

The road to La Cartuja slips gently between weeping willows and broom and disappears into the grey heart of the autumn afternoon.* Carpeted in dark green, the hillsides have a delicate sheen as they melt into the plain. Watery, magical and transparent, a heavy blue mist hangs over the countryside of Castile. No sharply defined colours on the heavy iron-plated ground. In the distance, square, severe towers of towns of noble lineage, now wounded and solitary in their grandeur.

*This Cartuja, or Charterhouse, at Miraflores on the outskirts of Burgos is one of the strongholds of the Carthusian order founded by Saint Bruno of Cologne in 1084. The buildings were completed in the late fifteenth century with the encouragement of Queen Isabel as part of her drive to consolidate Catholicism in Spain.

Over-arching sadness, ingenuous mountains, molten lead in a major key; gentle textures and softly glimmering, iridescent ash over the horizon. On both sides of the road massive trees, their foliage rustling and swaying before the landscape's ineffable bitterness. From time to time, the wind strikes up a solemn, monotonous march, silenced by the dry sound of withered leaves.

A band of women wearing bright red skirts walks by. A pointed gate, mottled by the sun, looms above the road like a triumphal arch ... The path twists and La Cartuja appears in all its funereal attire. The landscape displays its intensity in suffering, absence of sun, impoverished passion.

The black-edged city fans out the stripes of its poplar groves and shows off its Gothic monster of a cathedral, the work of a giant goldsmith, silhouetted against glorious purple. Although full of water, the river gives the impression of having run dry; clumps of trees are like smudges of old gold; ploughed fields unfurl straight-lined pentagrams and meld into the damp hues of the horizon. This silent, ascetic landscape has the charm of sorrowing religiosity. The eternal hand spilt only melancholy here. Every shape expresses terrible disillusion and desolation. The vision of God in this landscape is one of enormous fear. Everything is in awe, terrified and cowed. The people's wretched souls express their anguish in their speech, in their slow, serious gait, in their horror of the devil, in their superstition. Rusty crosses stand guard over every path; in churches, Christs stand in filthy holes, adorned with glass beads, grimy ex-votos and locks of hair singed by time, which peasant prayers invoke

entrance to la Cartuja

with the tragic faith of fear. A harrowing landscape of souls and fields …!

La Cartuja rises up in the midst of this solemnity, the bearer of general anguish. In the spacious square that precedes it, a cross with a swollen-bellied Christ strikes a grimly meditative note … La Cartuja is a mansion of shadows anointed by the surrounding cold. The body of the church

reredos by Gil de Siloé, La Cartuja

soars above it all, crowned by simple pinnacles and a cross. The rest is stone, half-gilded and undecorated. Three squat arches give access to a large whitewashed door where one must knock.

The door opens and a Carthusian appears against the light, his white woollen habit as pale as marble, with a huge beard covering his chest. The door squeaks mutedly and we enter the courtyard. The light is gentle and sparse. A white sculpture of a sentimentally majestic Saint Bruno stands in the centre between rose-bushes and ivy. To the left, the church's façade has strong, virile lines; the Calvary on its tympanum seemingly expresses primitive sorrow. In each corner brushstrokes of damp green float in the icy air. The monk takes us into the church, a snow-white tomb for kings and princes, a divine set-piece of medieval feats. In the background, the fine reredos recreates figures of richly adorned saints including a grim, horrendous Christ carved by Siloé: collapsed belly, vertebrae sticking out of skin, torn hands, strange curly hair, eyes sunk in death and a gelatinously pallid brow ... Next to him strong, impassive evangelists and apostles, scenes from the Passion as rigid as a corpse, and, holding the Cross on high, a proud, forbidding Eternal Father and a stout young man with the face of an idiot.

Over Christ's head, the white pelican of the Eucharist, and to complete the ensemble, angelic choirs, medallions, royal coats-of-arms, intricate lacework on the arch with a whole fauna of unknown saints and animals. The reredos has a single expression of grief: Christ. The rest is divinely executed, but says nothing. The figure of the Redeemer seems full of the tragic mysticism of the moment, but can find no resonance in the world of sculptures around him. It is very remote from passion and love; only he, amid general indifference and pride, overflows with lavish passion, charity and affliction. A magnificent reredos, such vibrant symbolism! At its feet, the grandiose tombs of the rulers of Castile, Juan I and his wife, in a conflagration of white marble. Their statues lie recumbent without a trace of death in their manner. The artist suffused their faces and expressions with an admirable portrayal of weariness and royal contempt. Their warm, transparent hands gird up rich robes studded with precious stones, overlaid with patterns of the most elegant flowers. Rosaries with large beads hang from their fingers, undulate over the folds of their cloaks and die over their feet. Their faces are turned to one side, as if they prefer not to see each other, in a rictus of supreme disdain.

The whole of Christian doctrine is set in stone around them: virtues, apostles and vices. Some alabaster figures loom aristocratically in the shadows; amusing little monks pray, curious men with open books, thoughtful faces and sensual lips, monkeys amid vines, lions on spheres, dozing dogs and ribbons and bowls of fruit, oranges, pears, apples and bunches of grapes. An enigmatic world of fantasy woven around defunct royalty. By their side another fine sepulchre, the Infante Don Alfonso, a gentle, funereally severe tone ... The light dims. Flames flicker opposite the ciborium. We smell strange damp and incense.

A clean-faced, bright-eyed monk appears in the choir, bows several times, opens his breviary and plunges into its pages. The monk accompanying me points to the delicate designs on the stalls. Footsteps spread concentric waves of sound through the air, fill the church with noise ... Pigeons flutter around the high windows.

Enclosed Order

After I had visited the church, the venerable monk took me to see a Saint Bruno on an odious little altar in a private chapel. 'This is Pereira's Saint Bruno,' he declared ... and reeled off a series of anecdotes concerning the work. The sculpture is no doubt well done, but is so lacking in expression! An eternally theatrical pose! The saint of silence and peace contemplates the crucifix he happens to be holding, as if looking at any old object. The effigy's stance communicates no spiritual suffering, no struggle against the flesh, no heaven-sent lunacy. It is a man ... and could be any man over forty bearing the mark of commonplace aches and pains ... In Spain we are forced to tolerate a quite intolerable stream of sculptures that inspire ecstasy in experts on technique, but don't evoke a single breath of emotion in their attitudes or expressions. They may be admirable re-creations, even admirable polychrome figures ... but the soul of the individual portrayed remains distinctly remote.

The saintly heroes of stories from long ago suffered romantically as a result of their love for God and humanity but were never reincarnated artistically. You only have to pay a visit to the galleries in the Valladolid museum! Quite horrific! It is true there are a very few successes ... but the rest ...

It is deeply depressing to see so many dismally mediocre sculptures. It is the most earthbound of arts. The geniuses in the field reached the first note on the spiritual scale ... They never managed a chord ...

Sculpture is a cold art, off-putting to the artist. His source of passion collides against the stone he carves ... He wants to breathe life into his figures and does so, wants to give them feeling and soul and does so ... but cannot open the sacred book of sweet subtlety within them where the rest of humanity can read emotions that would lead them into the solitary garden of dreams ... They reproduce ... never create ...

This saint is as coarse as a country bumpkin and as brawny as a Castilian villager, and seems to portray a down-trodden layman of old, one of the people who in the evening distrib-uted gruel to crowds of the poor worn down by hunger. What an impoverished idea on the part of poverty-stricken Señor Pereira, who imagined his Bruno driven mad by a sorrowing, quiet mysticism as the most vulgar of fellows after he has just had a bite to eat and gossiped a while ... Señor Pereira's imagination is most unfortunate, like the imaginations of all the other sculptors *exhibiting* in Valladolid, who portrayed their ideal, almost magical heroes as sturdy fools and village idiots ...

'Oh!' many will exclaim, 'Don't be so silly! They are splendid sculptures! Look at the wonderful hands! Observe the anatomical detail!' Yes, indeed, but it is the innermost things that convince me, I mean the soul they embody, so

S Bruno by Manuel Pereira, La Cartuja

that when we gaze at them our souls can feel at one with them. Generating the infinite copulation of artistic feeling and pleasurable pain that invades us when confronted by beauty ... I simply gazed upon this statue of Saint Bruno, so praised by lettered and unlettered alike, and felt nothing but deep Carthusian indifference. It is quite true the artist didn't intend to create a figure that leaves you untouched, but that was my reaction. That cold, blank expression in the face of the excruciating torture on the cross sums up the riddle of La Cartuja ... At least that's what I think ...

✤ ✤ ✤ ✤ ✤

'And as a result of circumstances that are not relevant here I succeeded in entering the enclosed area ...' The bearded, austere yet affable monk accompanied me.

We left the church ... The evening was already spreading its final shades of gold, rose and grey. The atmosphere was as becalmed as stagnant water in a wood. The light was gentle as if it were longing for the dawn. Words were whispered quietly like prayers at dusk ...

A small, squat door opened, and we entered the holy precinct of the cloister. This Cartuja in Miraflores has no inner exuberance. The passage exhibits a horrific collection of foul-coloured scenes of martyrdom ... The portrait of a monk placing a finger on his lips instils silence ... the passageway vanishes into milky brightness.

At the far end another passage appears lined with small doors opening out from starkly white walls, and a black painted wooden cross ... Humble solemnity, unnerving gravity and tense silence permeates these rooms. Everything is quiet, by order. Above these roofs, sky, pigeons and flowers, and above these, storms, rain and snow ... but the might of tortured minds imposes a dread tranquillity on these poor, whitewashed cloisters. We can hear nothing ... our offensive footsteps release distant echoes.

We halt occasionally and the oppressive quiet flows

tumultuously on … There is a whiff of quince as we pass by dark chambers. And of suffering and passions that have been all but stifled. Satan is sniffing around the solitary space. The silence in La Cartuja hurts. These men withdrew from life in order to flee its vices and passions. They came to hide the bitterness in their hearts in a reliquary of bygone poetry. They imagined a state of spiritual tranquillity, an enchanted lake where they would bury their desires and misery; but it wasn't to be … Their passions naturally blossomed again here in the most refined ways.

Solitude is a great hewer of minds. The man who entered La Cartuja a wreck submerged by life found no consolation.

We men are wretched, we want to be ruled by our bodies and subject material things to our bodies, but leave our souls out of account. These men bury their bodies here, not their souls. The soul goes wherever it wants. All our physical strength is in vain when we try to shift our soul from where it prefers to nail itself down. Besides … do we even know what our soul desires?

How painful and disturbing are these tombs of living men who swing like puppets in a torture chamber! How our hearts laugh and weep! Our souls welcome in admirable passions they can't then shake off. Eyes cry, lips pray, hands are wrung, but to no avail; the soul remains passionate, and these decent, miserable men seeking God in deserts of sorrow should realise how futile it is to scourge the flesh when the spirit craves something else.

These Carthusians are great cowards. They isolate

themselves because they long to live near God ... I wonder, which God these Carthusians are seeking. It cannot be Jesus ... No, no ... If these men made unhappy by life's hard knocks were inspired by Christ's teaching, they would take to the path of charity, not of empty, selfish, ice-cold penitence. Nothing is gained through prayer, just as nothing is gained through mortification. In our prayers we ask for what can never be granted. We see or would like to see a distant star, but it erases what is external, what is all around. The only path is charity, love for one's neighbour.

The soul suffers equally whether in a state of penitence or a state of charity; hence these men who deem themselves Christians shouldn't flee the world, as they do, but should enter there and help others in their misfortunes, console in order to be consoled, preach good works and spread peace. Such selflessness would make them real Christs in the ideal Gospel. La Cartuja is truly anti-Christian. All the love God commanded us to show is completely lacking: they don't even love one another. They speak briefly, only on Sundays, and come together solely to pray and to eat. They're not even brothers. They live in isolation ...

And all that so as not to sin ... That's why they don't speak! As if sin didn't exist in intimate meditation! As I said previously, they want to be bodies without blemish, because the soul, the soul can endure all kind of mortification. These wretches we must all pity think they can deceive themselves and deceive their senses by torturing the flesh. Who can ever guarantee that one, if not all, doesn't feel desire or love for the far-off women who are the reason they came there in the first place; or that they don't hate or despair ...? They worship before a Christ like Pereira's Saint Bruno, and weep and invoke heavenly spirits, but their souls love, desire and hate ... and their flesh remains rampant ... and at night in bed many of these men who are young and vibrant with life see visions of women they loved, people they scorned, that they still love and scorn and try to close eyes that refuse to close ... because we men cannot channel our souls to that lake we seek where neither anguish nor desire exist. These admirable resolute men flee the madding crowd, thinking sin hides there, and fall into a place that encourages thought, therefore sin. They fall into a garden primed for good and evil and enjoy great passion, though they flee such things. The great passion of silence.

They die here draining the cup of spiritual suffering, and do no good works ... Perhaps they do good to themselves ...? I doubt it: if they had drained their tears amid the wretched of this world, they would bring to the other realm a tree of mercy blooming with the white roses of those memories; in fact they die, never having tasted the spiritual wonder derived from good works done ... Besides, we know not why we are here ... Does God make us suffer? Then we shall suffer ... we have no choice.

But sometimes I think you are making a clever protest against God himself when you flee the world he created and seek out another, a quiet and serene god ... but can't because the cruelties refined by his sorrow that lodge in our hearts persist within us unto death ...

This silence is so oppressive! Everybody sees Carthusian

silence, peace and tranquillity. I see only anxiety, restlessness and formidable passions throbbing in these cloisters like a huge heart. The soul feels the desire to love and to love in a frenzy and the desire for another soul to fuse with ours ... and a desire to cry out to those miserable men meditating in their cells and tell them that the sun and moon, women and music exist; to cry out, arouse them and rescue their souls that inhabit the darkness of prayer, let them sing something optimistic and joyful ... but the silence prays a plainchant of Gregorian passion.

As we cross a cold, austere room, we see a Virgin in her heavenly cloak embroidered with stars, with a happy little child, wearing her lofty imperial crown ... something that recalls the month of May ... religious joy within Carthusian sadness.

We see no one in the spacious rooms and hear dripping damp and smell strange wax and shadowy arbours.

And yet more silence, silence and great sensuality ... The terrible nightmares of men in flight from temptations of the flesh who have embraced the twin aphrodisiacs of silence and solitude ...!

We walk through the noble, dignified refectory with its pulpit for fire-and-brimstone readings about martyrdoms and models of piety ... the white goblets and worn tables have a chaste air ... Red curtains let in the light and give the space a sombre, ruddy hue ... more empty passages, and then the great courtyard of La Cartuja.

A corner of the courtyard, where the monks are buried, is lined by scary, enigmatic cypresses. A rusty cross, the colour of gold, rises in the centre. A large blue shadow spreads its melancholy.

Withered roses and honeysuckle romantically drape the walls. Willows weep through elegant, funereal branches. There are cultivated gardens, pear and apple trees ...

A large, central fountain sings a watery melody, sighs timidly ... weeds hang down and lick the stone ... A cracked figurehead smiles an almost obliterated smile ...

On the back wall, next to the cemetery, an explosion of ivy ... Evening falls warmed by gentle, intimate hues ... We retraced our steps to emerge in the courtyard in front of La Cartuja ... Everything was bathed in a wonderful pink. Tranquil nature presides.

The bell chimed for the Angelus in solemn harmonies ... The monk knelt, crossed his hands and kissed the ground ... Two pigeons cooed under a hole on the roof ... It is a time when souls head towards eternity ... The wind whispers between branches and ivy leaves shiver and spiral ... As we depart, distant vistas spread out sheets of infinite grey.

SAN PEDRO DE CARDEÑA

❖ ❖ ❖ ❖ ❖

Echoes of Castile fall on the cool spring air. Spiders glitter on mounds of sweet-smelling corn and the sun extends opaque panes of red glass onto distant mists ... The trees resound like the sea and the glare of the sun strangely enamels the vast, solitary plain. Profound tranquillity invades the villages; silken threshing floors smell of flaxen incense and a gentle, almost priestly tinkle of bells accompanies resigned toil ... a fountain perpetually kisses the water channel that swallows it ... Cheerful ragamuffins shout out in the soft shadows of elms and walnut trees, scaring off the hens ... silent towers, their roofs riotous gardens; shuttered houses, all sadness and humility ... and a boy singing as he returns from the corn fields ...

Women are washing in a pool that is like a slab of green marble; their hair unkempt like Gorgons', they laugh and banter ...

The sublime unity of the lands of Castile is expressed by a single, solemn hue. Everything has Carthusian austerity, tedious homogeneity, self-questioning anxiety, authentic religiosity, solemn anguish, tender simplicity and numbing immensity.

The distant sierras are a blur of purple volcanic ash, some trees have souls of gold in the evening sun, and on far-off frontiers soft, dark colours open their huge fans and swathe the sweet, melancholy hills in iridescent velvet ...

Reapers' scythes bring death to fields of corn where poppy flowers set out their ancient cloth.

The red sky begins to resonate against the leaden backcloth; the wind abates and the vaguely mystical dusk of Castile intones a weary, eternal song ...

Carts clatter along tracks, insect string-musicians chirrup on the air; hay and anonymous flowers seem to burst from the chest hoarding their perfumes in order to caress the softness of the shadows ... as if an explanation of eternity might spring from an ineffable dialogue with the divine ...

The trees reflected in the water are surrounded by an exquisite autumnal melancholy ... and in damp, already dark valleys, sheep bleat to the monotonous jangling of a bell.

The landscape's rhythmic grandeur lies in the ruddy yellow which shuts out any other colour that attempts to interfere ... The dry grass carpeting the ground is still, and a spartan tower, windows gaping and empty, sticks its head, wearied by the years, between walnut trees and elms.

✤ ✤ ✤ ✤ ✤

The sun spreads transparent green waters over the meadow where Doña Sol and Doña Elvira once chatted.

the chevet of S Pedro de Cardeña

Silence brings religious depth to the stone's sense of history, disturbed only by the soft flap of pigeon wings.

Wooed by ivy and swallows, the whole monastery opens disconsolate, empty eyes and crumbles slowly, allowing ivy and blossoming willows to grow over ...

The luminous rays of the evening sun garland elms and walnut trees in yellow blooms, while the distant bright green turns bronze.

Swarms of greasy flies buzz melodiously; birds swoop frantically and settle on poplars that are like candelabra ready-made in the darkness.

Large tomb-like slabs embedded in nettles and purple flowers rise up in the great courtyard in front of the monastery.

To one side of the great building, a small entranceway with broken steps, a tower with a blackened coat of arms under hieratic, long-shanked, pink-beaked storks ...

Their large nests entangle their branches around the battlements.

A grandiose epic would like to clamour under the mysterious sun, but the crested helmets and chain-mail cuirasses long since retreated into the pitch-black distance ...

Jimena's loving figure, described in that wonderful tale, still seems to wait for her knight, who is driven more by his wars than her heart, and she will always wait like the Don Quixotes who await their Dulcineas, forever turning their backs on horrendous reality.

The story of that sterling love is told entirely in these lands; the melancholy of El Cid's wife passed this way ... her words of affectionate, passionate reproach resounded here, and are now dead ...

King of my soul and of these lands, my liege.
Why do you leave me? Where do you go? Oh where?

But heroes have to be heroes, and he moved the sweet figure aside, departing with his yeomen in search of death ... and the grieving, weeping woman paced through these cool willows and walnut trees until a white-bearded, shiny-pated holy man led her to her chamber and there she perhaps listened to the roosters every night ... And she desired and loved him because he was noble and strong, but to no avail, she only enjoyed his caresses for a few hours ...

Doña Jimena is the most feminine, entrancing note in the entire collection of Spanish ballads and is almost erased by her husband Rodrigo's swagger and aggression, but love's gentle charm wins out.

Jimena's giant love can be felt through the pages of the collection. A mature love and vibrant passion the spectre of duty forces her to stifle ... The dusty, rubbish-filled cloister is in the monastery next to the fountain of the martyrs ... and leads to the large, ugly church that has been profaned and the tomb of El Cid and his wife where their statues lie damaged and soulless, dripping with emeralds of damp ... The rest is a ruin where silvery slugs thread across nettles, rue, creepers and a thousand leaves on fallen stones ... all with a bitter, silent patina of damp ...

The storks stand so still and stiff they are like decorations appended to the turrets ...

A smell of meadows and antiquity. In the shadows from the swooning twilight, caressed by laden walnut trees, the monastery asks more questions, suggests more ...

El Cid & Doña Jimena, S Pedro de Cardeña

✤ ✤ ✤ ✤ ✤

When we leave this valley, the bright reflections from the sunset are extending over the flatlands … A plain of tawny gold crowned by a red halo, rusted silver battlements and in the sky a waxing, cold blue moon … Epic iron voices ring out over the countryside, loud, ghostly and blood-red, softened by Schumann's sorrowful evening song that wrenches at my soul.

SANTO DOMINGO DE SILOS

❖ ❖ ❖ ❖ ❖

The Journey

You must leave Burgos in one of those odious, uncomfortable cars that splutter anxiously under an enormous pile of suitcases and travel bags. The great bend opens up and the edge of the road disappears in rows of slender, rustling poplars.

It is a tranquil August day and the sun is drawing out the reddish hues of the countryside … A charming bright pink carpets some glades of broom, a whole gamut of blues suffuses trees and blood red screams from the sunken bellies of the undulating terrain; an infinite horizon reverberates with lead-grey thunderclaps. Sometimes the plain wants to express the spirit of the landscape, but gently sloping hills loom.

Amid trees and weeds, remnants of ancient crosses rise up in dead, desolate shadows … Villages pass by, sad, silent and bitterly passionate, their churches great blocks of stones, almost fortified towers, their apses silent … The car's horn hoots morosely, insulting the austere landscape and plunging us into a haze of shadows and bright pools of light.

Our car drives past a wonderful, splendidly isolated Renaissance palace shaded by lofty trees, with minimal balconies and magnificent wrought iron … Today it is abandoned and locked up, aloof and grandiose next to a garden of jasmine … A popular story immediately springs to mind … 'This,' they tell me, 'was the safe haven for a distinguished lady who seduced Philip II …' The palace turrets disappear behind foliage. The ribbon of the road silently unravels in blinding light … Of all the towers that file past, we are most moved by a lone grey stone fort on the way out of a village, straight out of a ballad of star-crossed love and fissured by the light burden of a fine cape of ivy. Tall, meagre poplars give the road a deathly aspect.

We can now relax as the car grumbles miserably off into the distance. We travellers have been dropped in the heart of Castile, surrounded by austere mountain ranges in the midst of an imposing, lofty landscape. Wraps of soft silk are scattered over the ground …

To reach Silos we must travel in a broken-down carriage, pulled by three wretched animals covered in sores on which flies feast. The other travellers were coarse people, stupid in their desperate rush to get on quickly and not lose their seats, oblivious to the solemn majesty of the horizon. Women carrying children in their arms, an unshaven priest with a greenish soutane, a young man wearing huge spectacles with the air of a seminarist and some dismal livestock-dealers.

They had nothing interesting to say; some dozed, while others chattered inanely ... The driver hurried the animals on, his amusing lilt full of gruff, manly harmonies. His manner was lordly to a degree. White clouds of dust billowed around the coach that occasionally slipped rapidly down slopes between grey clumps of dusty thyme, accompanied by the languid, sleep-inducing clatter of the halters.

Everybody remained silent inside the carriage. It was one of those meditative moments that occur on journeys when sleep casts out its invisible, honeyed chains, spilling its balsam over hearts, half-closing eyes in a spasm of bodily gratitude, dancing capriciously around heads ... Someone uttered a word, then shut up, silenced by the languid, soporific atmosphere. The priest snored beatifically, mouth half-open and belly heaving at a ridiculous rate; the bespectacled youth sighed like an effeminate monk, someone else stretched and a placid woman conjured a huge white, tremulously august breast out of the half-shadows of her dress and suckled a chubby blond babe who put her chaste rose of a little mouth to the dark, smoky nipple.

The driver burst into song at the top of his voice. I quivered in dismay. In this land of austere colour and light I thought I would find someone intoning a noble Castilian song at once mighty and serene. To my horror, rather than a drawn-out melody of Gregorian simplicity (a tone many songs have here) I was greeted by a frightful chorus from a tawdry Madrid musical. The coach-driver bawled out the notes, making an intolerable din. He interrupted the flow of my thoughts ... I could only curse the loathsome, criminal endeavours of certain Spanish music-makers ... Make melodies, if you will; but for the sake of God and his mother, don't pen coarse, vulgar ballads ...! The animals' jingling bells reach a crescendo and mercifully release me from that voice ... Golden hills soar upwards, scarred by round boulders and dark thyme.

The diligence takes a rest in a quiet little village with huge chimneys.

The square still preserves houses that have sunk into the ground, their original, admirable coats of arms now grimy and black. One house contained a forge and in that pitch-black den you could see the bright glow of red-hot coals and the workers' motionless, penetrating eyes. Out in the sun, children played with a dog. Hens huffed and puffed in a makeshift shelter. My travelling companions wake up, chatter and protest because we don't move off. Old and weary, one of the horses, which has a deeply sorrowful expression, sways its big head in resignation and closes its bleary eyes, bloodshot from the dust on the road, and tries quite involuntarily to inhale a breath of refreshing air. Wretched, hard-working hack, always travelling these roads in cruel winters and infernal summers! Who will ever believe you are nobler and worthier than these folk who are always making such a selfish fuss? Poor victim of our God, eternally condemned to ferry people who never spare you a glance! Who will believe you are better, holier and worthier of admiration than most men? Wretched, rotting flesh, a lowly acolyte in a trial of strength! You are so much more elegant and courteous than these cattle-dealers who sit next to me!

The humble, good-natured beast desperately shifts its whole body, frightening off flies that want to gorge on the deep welts on its back …

We returned to our onward trail and the landscape began to assume a savage splendour. Simple yet grandiose hills, rugged crags and strange red blotches.

Hontoria de la Cantera, on the Covarrubias road

The road snaked up the hill, swerved and dipped all of a sudden. Another moment of private meditation overtook the travellers. Moments when the landscape blurs into a single colour. Tranquil moments of sunny monotony. Anxious moments untouched by anxiety … The diligence airily descends sharp bends and enters a small and pleasant valley where we glimpse the red roofs of a town next to a river's gentle crystalline waters.

Covarrubias

The diligence turns into the first street, pursued by the curious looks of the locals. It passes a beautiful, solitary Byzantine cross and through a remarkable triumphal arch, the gateway into the town. The arch is a gilded, aristocratic, Renaissance wonder with large *repoussé* wrought-iron grilles and cornucopia, foliage and coats of arms for ornamentation. The coach stops by a door with a pointed arch topped by a small shield. This is the inn. The innkeeper doubles as the town's doctor. He cuts a strange figure, what with his eyes bulging out of their sockets, his Málaga-style haughty airs and restrained urbanity. He came out surrounded by his children and welcomed us pleasantly enough … On a table I spotted books by Pérez Zuñiga and Eduardo Marquina, this good gentleman's favourite authors.

This town has superb, vintage corners. The main street is narrow and dark, its ancient houses swollen and falling apart, with coats of arms over the most modest lintels. Brutal stone slabs triumphantly pave the ground. Ugly stunted women stand in doorways, eyes sunk into yellow, wrinkled skin. The men walk slowly along, all stooping shoulders and blackish faces. Human forms prop up the walls of the imposing colonnade, distressed quite unconsciously by an atmosphere that is simply off-putting. Your heart calls out to see a woman's pink, fresh cheeks. Young girls stroll down the street in voluminous, highly unfashionable skirts that exaggerate their hips, but their faces bear the imprint of tragic boredom.

The character of the main square is the stuff of legends of war. The palace of Count Fernán González dominates the background with its large pointed doorway and chivalric balconies. Artful paramour of ancient things, grass winds

town gate, Covarrubcás

a green ribbon around the abandoned ruin. Further to the right, the sooty arches of a colonnade begin.

A truncated pyramid stands by the road leading out of town, a large, grimy, silvery tower where rain has highlighted faded loops of gold, crimson red and topaz ... Doña Urraca's tower. Its only special feature is the resonance of popular myths that all these relics of antiquity purvey. The myth remains incomplete, or at least no one told me … They simply pointed and said, 'Little Infanta Doña Urraca was walled up in there by order of her father for a long time …' 'Why?' My gentleman companion hasn't the slightest idea.

I scent a fairy story. A medieval princess walled up by her father … Could it have been love? My gentleman companion guide didn't know, but it's better that way. The supremely romantic tower is now a pigeon-loft. Birds have nested in the roof of its devastated barbicans and are forever fluttering around. A tea rose would like to embrace the fort.

Further on, the small belfry of a chapel looms, sheltering the church. The church has this land's eternally Gothic arches; its strong lines meet and kiss at a rose-window; it has rather flat arches and the usual high windows. On walls dripping with damp, sepulchral monuments exhibit stiff, armoured knights, epitaphs, cherubs … The tombs of Fernán González's daughters are under the main altar, protected by an angel. The altar of the blessed martyrs Cosmas and Damian, the town's patron saints, stands in a chapel next to a ridiculous row of haughty Romanesque, Byzantine and Gothic sculptures set without rhyme or reason on a worm-eaten wooden plank. They look like two trite-faced dolls wrapped in faded damask, their wiry hair stuffed into huge, dusty hats. They are surrounded by ex-votos and a light weeps quietly in front of them. The parish priest declared that they were the favourite images of a town that had swamped them in religious fervour … An intense twilight gloom hit me. The town had invested its whole faith in these ill-made dolls, the

street in Covarrubías

toys of some giant's child ... The two absurd artefacts are the sum-total of this hapless town's vision of the infinite ... The other chapels house dusty saints in deplorable garb ... Beyond that is the great Flemish reredos of the Adoration of the Magi. Full of innocent grace and musical movement, the Virgin holds her Child on her knees so he can receive the pious offering from a black king whose elegant hands offer him a golden chalice ... The rest of the figures remain outside the focus of the scene. They are simply observers. The only dialogue is between sweet Mary's eyes and the black monarch of childish dreams ...

The large sacristy contains softly coloured paintings and chests of drawers. There is the odd Flemish interior wonderfully lit as if by Vermeer ... The sun directs its golden beams at the cloister full of withered grass. The tracery on the arches weaves patterns on the scorched ground ...

A strong smell of bread floods the street. Young women flounce by whispering. The river recreates a bridge ... The poplars nod their heads.

The Mountain

We meander down magically sinuous little streets, past houses sunk into brown-grey earth, wafted along by warm odours from the stables, and chance upon a secluded corner and the profound silence of a closed church. To return to the main square we walk down a narrow, depressing street where a sign on a house declares: 'The divine Vallés was born here.' A bulky lady dressed in black, with large, silly, bluish eyes, shouted by way of explanation, 'Yes, the divine Vallés, the divine Vallés, Philip II's doctor …' We thank her for that information, cross the square and reach the inn.

We have to take the carriage again to go up to Silos. The steep slope we must climb begins immediately we leave the town … The river's lunar bluish silver melds into the dark green of the trees reflected in its watery, enigmatic depths. White clouds flower continuously in the sky and vary the tone of the sun's melody … The coach struggles up the slope. The driver doesn't bother to chide his animals. The sun pours down its molten fire.

The red roofs of Covarrubias gradually recede into the beautiful harmony of the landscape. Doña Urraca's funeral tower strives to see itself in the river. Humid shadows cloak its banks …

We soon reach the mountains. The peaks vie against one another. The first looks wild, full of thyme and holm-oaks, some loom further on, grey and pale purple, and others blend their violet into the horizon.

The carriage advances slowly up the road that encircles the bellies of the foothills like a huge ring. The opaque, austere landscape shimmers. Majestic wildness rules. There are huge screes of red stones, giant claws coated in dusty velvet moss. The trees dance, cavorting barbarically over precipices.

The wind howls dramatically through these mountains … A strong wind, laden with wonderful aromas. A gently pleasant, biblically solemn wind. A wind out of stories of wandering souls and wolves. A wind with an eternally wintry soul, accustomed to barking dogs and whistling round crags at the mysterious, midnight hour. A wind full of folk poetry, the frightening delights of which grandmother recounted when she told us her tales ...

It slaps me hard on the face, wipes its icy cold all over me ...

Retuerta, on the Silos road

As we trundle along, great spurs of holm-oaks stick out from the slopes, bluish grass eddies, sweet junipers sway over precipitous inclines.

Wondrous mirages surge above the dusty bracken around medieval cities, walls of gorgeous gold like enchanted castles in stories about witches, evocations of buildings from the ancient Orient, sombre remnants of the tragedies of war ... As our perspective changes, new cities of stone appear, the thickest of walls where Ramayanic cubes protrude ... walls with stone doors like the tomb of Darius near Naqsh-e Rustam, mournful and grandiose like that monument. Imperially luxurious, magnificent stairways arise occasionally from the stony flames of the rocks, born out of an abyss and leading to an unknown, impossible place ... The road keeps unwinding its serene ribbon. The colour grey exhausts even its most unusual shades. A bright green sea sweeps along the floor of some ravines.

In the valleys we cross, the wheat shines and glints, brimming with sun. The most remarkably coloured villages pass by, slender romantic belfries and red roofs over dark, gloomy houses. In one small dip a village reclines gracefully on the mountainside, smiling ingenuously. Massive, sturdy, century-old walnut trees rhyme their bronze hues with the bright red earth. Poor plantations follow and broad glens overgrown with briars. It seems like an imitation of a child's drawing … Other villages are born from summer greenery and flaunt bell-towers that resemble disfigured Christs.

Distant trees and cypress groves look like Gothic towers foreshortened by pale inks.

The rustic exuberance of the mountains re-appears. Capers spring from enormous crevices like green waterfalls frozen on the rocks. Strange alphabets pattern the ground and gigantic walls. Faces and scenes are drawn on rocks. Rounded pebbles long to roll down slopes to the dark red calm of the gullies. Small woods of broom provide dark purple haunts for lizards. Snakes open the mouths of their lairs in forgotten crannies.

The carriage runs along, its jangling bells jarring the divine peace, frightening quails that fly up in panic and driving away the ghastly toads meditating on the roadside.

Silent processions of purple-bodied pines wind down into the abyss from the highest peaks, heads stuffed with visions of twilight.

Stones spring from the ground, smooth and polished like the skulls of buried giants. The slopes are awash with lyrical springs of yellow flowers, iridescent roses, blossomy foam surges ...

And more holm-oaks ... and more junipers ... and more pine-trees and more gusty caresses from the wind.

in a valley near Covarrubias

High poplars bedecked with bells that Góngora jangled so pleasantly rustle in *rubato*. After several interludes of inner tranquillity an ancient monastery came into sight. A church tower arose above a village's fortified buildings; from the road it looked like a grey stone monstrance in a holy procession or a large glass of balsam like those Leonardo da Vinci's genius placed in the hands of his Mary Magdalenes.

The village slumbers in a gentle valley ... below crags that threaten to collapse and bury it.

The Monastery

Fortified walls enclose the clump of houses. The monastery is on the inside.

Its entrance is ugly and out of proportion. When we knocked, a grimy, ragged lay figure opened the door. He had a humble, womanly air ... We were ushered into a great stone courtyard full of gilded desolation, shockingly cold in its artistry. We think this entrance to monkish life must be the entrance to its renowned Romanesque cloister. The effect is unpleasant. Finally we are offered some hospitality ...

The cell is white and shadowy with a modernist crucifix and an ink-stained wooden table. In one corner the bed hides its whiteness behind the curtains. An evocative, magical mountain wind blows through the half-opened window ... Now and then the rustle of monks' habits rushing through the gallery breaks the silence. Night is about to fall. The monastery's bronze bell chimes and its echoes ring around the distant mountains ... Two huge dogs in the first courtyard prepare to howl at midnight ... Outside the cell we saw a gallery where shadows danced rhythmically. It led to a grey stone staircase overlooked by colossal and quite miserable figures of saintly monks in black habits with gilded crosiers and absurd crowns, in front of which a sacred red light burnt disconsolately. There was a fear of colour in these stony depths ... A muffled sound of habits, clattering rosary beads, mysterious whispers, chromatic scales of footsteps that went silent in deep purple and silences that seemed faintly anxious

... The light escaping through the high windows precipitated cascades of shadows in passages and chambers ...

When I entered my cell, it was flooded by the full moon ... I shut the door ... and was surrounded by sonorous silence. My soul tried to meditate, but the holy horror inspired by the tranquillity of the passion prevented that. It was an experience I'd never had before and only involuntary contemplation was possible. The roses of our inner world open in these realms of silence and when they exhale their scent we inevitably slip into the honey of spiritual confusion ...

The full moon was still entering my room. When I got into bed I had the tragic impression I was imprisoned by that solitary pallor ...

The dogs soon began their barking and miserable lamentations, voices that sounded prophetic in the silence. They were clamouring sorrowfully, perhaps against their own bodies and lives, thick, guttural howling that stirred fear that quaked and trembled, sounds out of the deepest corners of their souls, like actors soliloquising in a grand tragedy that only the moon can feel as it promenades its romantic, feminine light between the stars. Lamentations of passionate souls intoxicated by infinite pain, darkly questioning a cold, impassive spirit. Gloomy harmonies sung with thunderous, inhuman grief, apocalyptic screams of men tortured in dungeons, funeral curses with a biblical accent, Dantesque chords searing the heart ... Symbolic chaos from a life of thought ... Those howls strike panic in us like something from beyond the grave. We don't recognise the emotion sweeping through us, simply understand that sound is not

entirely uttered by an animal and can only think a super-
natural spirit resides in the horrible musical crescendo ...
The howl starts as a shrill, sorrowful, stuttering cry like
human sobbing, then firmly embraces the bass scream of
hellish torment ... and that dog is afraid, very afraid, when
it howls; it pricks up its ears, shudders, half-closes its eyes
in a malevolently satanic scowl and inner turmoil prompts
it to break into an ululation. Premonitions of the anguish
latent in other worlds invade us when we hear the distress
in that howl and our hair stands on end. It is a sardonic curse
from afar, and most horrible ... that we'd rather not hear and
... we feel hemmed in, alone ... and want to run and sing
but are pursued by the dramatic force of that terrible dirge
plucked on the lyre of fear, that at times wants to break out
in black sounds from the abyss and at times to strike an
unheard level in the strange gamut of fears.

In a new Theogeny imagined by the marvellous, admirable
Maurice Maeterlink, the dog would be a benign soul, the
progeny of a magic horse and a curious virgin, one coveted
by Death so she can proclaim her victory over men ... and
the faithful dog, friend of humans, would suffer terribly,
but would artfully herald the Pale One ... Death comes and
orders the dogs to sing her song ... Sensing her presence,
they shout, don't want to obey her, but she digs in her spurs
of invisible silver and the howling begins. It is the only way
to explain how such a noble, peaceful animal can cry out with
such terrifying, lethal solemnity ... Yes, it is death, death,
that stalks these halls with her huge blood-spattered scythe
the dogs can see in the moonlight ... it is the inevitability

of death that floats across these halls searching for its next victims, death is the thought filling us with anguish via the howl of malediction ... Death leads souls into enigmatic, impossible solitude ... The dogs (beings from unfamiliar mythology) glimpse deception or truth and howl drawn-out majestic howls in a deep timbre that surges from the abyss, on a tide of luxurious, Asiatic fear ...

The dogs are still howling ... Yellow candlelight triggers waves of uncanny shadows on the cell's high, white walls and live heartbeats that thump all around. Sometimes it feels as if the ceiling wants to crash down in the distant, opaque light ... The dogs are locked into their tragedy. Perhaps driven by religious superstition, someone tries to silence them from a window ... my soul knows intense fear. Words about howling dogs stir inside me, written by the mad, magical Count of Lautréamont. Two large turquoise shards of light slip gently into my room.

❖ ❖ ❖ ❖ ❖

The following morning, I was woken by the monks' beautiful chanting and the dogs' fierce barking. By now death had forsaken them. I walked along splendidly light galleries, past monks who greeted me affably. It was a magnificent summer morning with a mountain flavour. The light had a sharp shade of blue when I entered the impressive Romanesque cloister. It is impossible to give a sense of the way you leap into history the second you enter this place with its living antiques and romantic tales of monks and warriors. The cloister is charged

in the monastery church, Silos

with emotions from the past, its stone etched with stories
of artistic torment. It is squat and profound, muscular and
moving. The rhythms of a raw, brutal, austerely expressive
age suffuse its sad and graceful galleries. The manly, severe
arches attempt to disappear into a background of sparse,
profound blackness. The light is a gentle blue.

'Byzantine' Virgin & Child, Silos

An immense, brightly painted Byzantine Virgin sits at the end of one gallery. She sits on a throne holding the Child on her knees. Virgins of this kind always display a naïvety, emblematic of worthy religiosity ... but this dignified example is portrayed with savage frankness. And the huge image creates an eerie silence as her head touches the ceiling and her gawping eyes look nowhere, with rigid, over-large hands of that era ... They bury their monks beneath the cloister floor ... we see signs of burials betrayed by a single letter ... Further along the gallery with the Byzantine image, Saint Dominic's ancient sepulchre rests on two capricious lions. Opposite is the ugliest of chapels, which seems to provoke protests from the great works in the cloister. Its altarpiece is a huge print of a chubby, winsome blond Catalan Heart of Jesus, showing off his brand new loutish haircut and trimmed beard fresh from the barbers.

Whenever you gaze at the awe-inspiring series of arches, an ancient, majestic chord explodes in your soul ... The usual, whimsical stone slabs cover the ground. There are consoling, ineffable patches of damp ... An equally horrific, offensive fountain (the modernist variety) hums a soothing tune in the centre of the courtyard, the former cemetery. The spiritual wonder of a cypress soars up, eager to kiss the nearby belfry. Then more trees, beds of yellow flowers and shady grass in the small garden ...

A Castilian knight sleeps on one cloister wall, the hero from a beautiful love epic. The wisest of monks tells us his story. The legend that took place in the lands of Castile had the usual protagonists ... A brave, generous knight, an aristocratic Moorish friend, the wives of both ... Then lavish weddings, wars and the final tragedy; a love of friendship that triumphs over patriotic love ... The legend issues strong and calm from the monk's passionate lips and his melancholy eyes twinkle with joy at the artistic illusion he has spun.

Thousands of strange, unfamiliar scenes are painted on that original and unusual ceiling in a range of colours, mainly red, white and grey, that the passage of time has dimmed and blurred. The beams are also painted, with exotic shapes that are difficult to interpret. Some are imaginary animals, bulls, griffins, lions, bats, cabbalistic signs and contorted lines. There is the odd grotesque, religious scene of a distinctly profane nature ... A mass celebrated by a donkey, helped by another animal as an acolyte. The celebrant wears a chasuble and other garments. A black cross hangs in the background. Other scenes are amusing and less shocking. The witty irony and caustic humour of the paintings contrast with the imposing capitals that top stumpy, long-suffering columns.

These strikingly large capitals are in harmony with the whole and constitute the cloister's artistic epiphany ... They reveal an era when sense of line scaled a remarkable peak of strength and understanding. The drawings are soberly complex, a fine, orderly forest of amusingly morbid lines ... The gilded stone is an array of green stems, artistic tracery and delicate filigree. Each capital is a huge precious stone, but not one that sparkles. The carving is magnificent. The capitals carry rare leaves, various acanthuses, exotic creepers, warm trellis, unknown mythical plants and stylised veget-ables. Most have representations of animals. In Ávila I had

capital with harpies, Silos

already seen two pelicans with necks lovingly and strangely entwined in a vibrant spasm, but had never seen representations of such madness on a Romanesque capital. Perhaps because I had never seen one so close up: the truth is I was astonished by the scenes of infinite torture that I now witnessed. Nightmarish harpies with owls' bodies, eagles' wings, women's heads lurk amid the stems and leaves on some capitals ... and the birds peck one other, join mouths and clash wings in horrendous inversions expressed in unlikely forms … In other scenes one weird animal mounts the next, bites another's tail with lustful relish in satanic sexual acts practised by frightening trinities of tortured flesh.

Some, surely among the last to be carved, depict human figures, symbolic representations and scenes from Biblical history. At the four corners of the cloister there are bas-reliefs in which large, lovely, remotely Italianate angels protect a Virgin, and scenes from the life of Jesus. He appears in oriental garb, hair and beard made of small, stiff curls like an Assyrian priest's.

The figures on the bas-reliefs display the melancholy majesty of primitive dance, the liturgical solemnity of sacred rites, disturbingly hieratic as in visions of heaven … The gentlest light floods the cloister above …

Two novices emerge from that light and walk close-by. One's face is intelligent and the other's is brutish … They are oblates.

We walk to the upper cloister that has a monkish array of big saints, old paintings and photographs … A bell rings solemnly. The monks cross the gallery on their way to the choir … They disappear through a door, hiding under their austere and graceful cowls.

※ ※ ※ ※ ※

It is time for high mass. The muffled steps of the monks making their way along passageways and galleries … A bell tolls slowly … The tranquil morning light spreads magnificently over the bulk of the monastery. The cypress receives a divine breath of sun ... The deserted Romanesque cloister echoes resonantly. The monks process through the beautiful door that leads to Saint Dominic's tomb. Austere cowls still conceal their heads.

I accompany them into the church. It is a huge, cold, poorly appointed, unpleasant place. It has no altarpieces, images or colour. A martyred Saint Sebastian is venerated on the main altar in a display of artless nudity. Funeral candles from the town's families litter the floor. The church is damp and deserted ... two or three emaciated old men stare vacantly and cough occasionally, alarmed by the lugubrious echo that then rings out.

The choir emerges from behind a sturdy iron grille.

I sit in the pews in the form of a choir between laymen and oblates ... The ceremony begins. The abbot takes his high seat of honour that looks down on two black rows of monks. All start by greeting the Catholic Trinity, bend their bodies low, remaining stooped until they have finished the last Gloria. Then they sit down, stand up, remove their hoods and put them back on in a remarkable rhythm, a tragically solemn theatricality that expresses the immense power of ancient liturgy. There is a short pause while the ministrants who will sing the mass leave. They walk very slowly across the church preceded by novices with thuribles that bear no resemblance to the hands of the acolytes in Verlaine's subtle verse. The priests wear cowls as white as their gowns, which show off the rich, bright silvery green of their chasubles. The altar awaits them, with flickering, divine candles and an immaculately religious mantel with humble lace trim.

The monks officiating are men with weather-beaten complexions who walk at an indecent pace, their black, impure hands bristling with tufts of hair, men nature has cruelly punished. Surely the altar will totter. If only for aesthetic reasons these men should not be allowed to sing mass, touch the sacred, exalted chalice and raise the sublime host, symbol of purity and universal peace. Women should perform these priestly tasks, with hands like pink madonna lilies, immersed in a sea of white lace, hands fit to raise the host and give the blessing, irises with true priestly charms and mouths that could rest on the chalice like gentle, passionately pure garnet stones, the only lips properly initiated by their beauty or symbolic meaning to receive the ineffable mystical harmonies of the celestial Lamb's blood. It is an ugly act when these gross, burly men dip their lips into the pristine light emanating from that mysterious sacrifice.

The priests reach the altar and commence their moving, resonant Gregorian chant.

The monks gently bow their heads over their breviaries. They are engulfed in an abyss of austere music. Light pours through the high windows. A majestic melody issues from every breast in the same grave rhythm and bass tone. The melody has no resolution, like a huge black marble column disappearing into the clouds. It is at once jagged and smooth, profound and vaguely intimate. The voices visit every shade of melancholy through the magical world of the keys. A cathedral surfeit of gravity imbues the chant ... The notes begin a strange, capricious dance, avoiding any sentimental harmony. The Gregorian chant strives to give an impression of grandeur, stern austerity, inner spirituality, of extolling the divinity with a voice devoid of passionate intensity. The melody wants to soar above all existing things. Wants to create serene canticles of praise far from tragedies of the heart. Flees any emotional pitch. There are huge breaths when one syllable goes from note to note that never reach the anticipated resolution … The Gregorian chant in Silos inhabits an atmosphere of great feeling. These melodies, spoken in unison and without music, are sung here to the accompaniment of an organ that has the softest, most harmonious timbres … and, of course, there is intense individual feeling in the monkish voices amid the musical penumbra from the organ. It is a festive day and solemnity is sparingly present in the ceremonials … The sacred dances of the ministrants resonate in the choir. The priests embrace and the monks follow suit. They sing an *Agnus Dei* with a lilting, ancient melody… The mass ends on a solemn crescendo from the choir. Their strong, beautiful voices want to raise the roof in the clouds of chords released by the organ … The poor laymen, uncouth, happy-go-lucky fellows, sing with extreme religious unction. The ceremony ends and the monks process to Saint Dominic's sepulchre that is set on that dreadful altar. There they kneel and pray.

The fetters from redeemed slaves of old still hang from the walls.

I walk through the vast rooms of the monastery filled with paintings of sacred scenes accompanied by a kind and pleasant monk. He is the organist. He expresses himself with an appealingly unpretentious innocence. He shows me the reliquary containing wonderful blue and gold enamelled boxes and bones of saints; I see Saint Dominic's chalice, a huge silver goblet adorned with oriental filigree and the magnificent paten studded with colourful gems ...

We walk down a broad gallery. There is a large, laughable marine painting in one corner: a tall vessel rides the raging waves with two ladders at the ready to let people on board. In the foreground a monk points to a ladder up which other monks are clambering ... My friend explains: 'That was the symbolic representation of his order's pledge. The monk standing at the foot of the vessel was our Father Saint Benedict, inviting souls to enter the monasteries of his order. The sea is the world with all its disappointments and sorrows, the boat is eternal salvation.' I remained silent and contemplative. 'You should know,' continued my companion, 'that all of us who belong to Benedictine communities are saved by the simple fact we are religious men ... that was our holy founder's pledge.' I exclaimed, 'Well, I can't think why your houses aren't packed with believers ... it is a beautiful pledge'... The monk smiled sceptically ... 'Ay, my friend, these are evil times!' ... we continued meandering down the passageway.

Then we talked about music. The poor fellow was only familiar with plainchant. He had entered the monastery as a child and had not left since.

He was ignorant of sublime orchestral symphonies, had never savoured the cello's deep romanticism, never shivered at the horn's smouldering rage ... was only familiar with the secret of the organ, and then only to service the archaic Gregorian chant ... I mentioned Beethoven, whose immortal name sounded as if for the first time in his ear, and then said, 'I'm a very poor musician and not at all sure I can remember a fragment of this music that is unfamiliar to you, but let me sit at the organ and see if I ...'

We walked across the empty church, climbed narrow, dusty stairs and entered the organ loft ... At my suggestion, the brother sang the *Agnus Dei* they had spoken during the mass, now with organ accompaniment. It was frankly sublime ... My friend sang slowly, placidly, at a quiet, almost pastoral pitch.

I then sat at the organ. There were the mystical keys with a yellow patina, rows of imaginary pages awaking at their sound and registers to shape divine assemblies of voices ... The monk blew the bellows. That very second I remembered a work of inhuman sorrow, a pathetic love lament, the *allegretto* from the Seventh Symphony. I played the first chord and entered the anguished percussion of its constant, nightmarish rhythm.

I hadn't played three bars when the monk who had recounted the legends in the cloister appeared in the doorway ... He was extremely pale. He came over, put his hands over his eyes and exclaimed most sorrowfully, 'Play on, play on!'... but perhaps God was being merciful: I reached the point when the music takes on an accent full of the passionate pain of love, and my fingers stumbled on the keys and the organ went silent. I couldn't remember any more ... The monk's passionate eyes looked into some remote place. Eyes that bore all the bitterness of a spirit aroused from a fictitious illusion, searching for an ideal that has perhaps been lost forever. The glinting eyes of a Spaniard sheltering under brows that have begun to turn snowy grey. Intelligent eyes full of emotion, eternal conflict ... When the organ ceased to sob, he left without saying a word and disappeared down the stairs ... The organist exclaimed, 'Things on his mind!'... And laughed and tittered stupidly; he had understood nothing of what had just happened. We came down from the organ loft. As we left the church, the atmosphere felt alive, palpitated: it was a huge book that had closed on the lectern.

✣ ✣ ✣ ✣ ✣

Time passes calmly, peacefully.

The brothers walk past one another in the cloisters as they go about their tasks. Lay brothers are digging in the kitchen garden. A novice learning the organ plays distant chords. Inside, the atmosphere never changes. It is time to eat, a bell rings and we all head to the dining room. At the threshold, the affable abbot washes our hands in a gesture of respect and deference towards the pilgrim.

When we walk in, the monks are in their rightful places. The abbot presides from his wooden throne. They all stand.

The dining room is dark and magnificent with two black columns in its centre. There are no tablecloths. You can breathe the poverty-stricken grandeur. The abbot lowers his eyes and exclaims, *'Benedicite'* and they all answer, *'Benedicite'*... followed by the psalm. They bow and repeat those glories with a funereal rattle. Silence descends for a *Pater Noster* ... then from the depths of the refectory someone prays in a delicate, piping voice ... and when he finishes they all lugubriously respond, 'Amen' … and sit down to eat. A lay brother enters late; he can't have heard the bell. He kneels before the abbot, his hands clasped over his chest, and bows his head with the pitiful gesture of a man who is poor. The Superior blesses him casually, as if puffing out air, and the wretched old man withdraws to eat.

An emaciated, jaundiced yellow youth, his head long and misshapen, appears in the white pulpit. He crosses himself, opens a venerable tome and begins to read.

The book tells the story of an ancient father of the Church … The devil who eternally tempts hermits … A fierce struggle against the invisible enemy they think comes from outside, not noticing that he is hiding deep, deep within their hearts … The saint in the story tortures himself in order to attain the infinite. He abandons everything to devote himself to inner contemplation … but temptation arises from that admirable mysticism … and under his bed he sees green, yellow-eyed monsters and in his nightmares contemplates fiery serpents with heads of mice and horrible, vicious lizards … A life of appalling torture. The Middle Ages live on in the monk's tale. The saint flees from his visions of hell and spends his nights in a vigil, a prey to fearful fanaticism, in the dark, tragic solitudes of a church, beating his breast, embracing a Christ … His hero's natural unhinging guides his imagination to divine paths of celestial visions … and he is swept aloft by wonderful angels and amid the clouds sees the Almighty's supreme majesty on his throne of suns with an affable Father Christmas face, and speaks to a most sweet, holy Mary of Nazareth on her path of flowers under a cascade of starry light. One day the admirable saint fell asleep. His companions didn't succeed in waking him: night came and they saw the sleeping man levitate and remain in the air for a long time. Then he descended, woke up and told them what he'd seen in his epiphany. He dreamt angels took him to beautiful landscapes among the clouds where his spirit tried to abandon his body ... but couldn't because that was the decree of the Lord, and the angels returned him to Earth, and the saint wept ... What happened in the tale was most magical and literary ... decapitated heads returning to their place, apparitions from old monasteries that have long since disappeared ... resonances from primitive faith. The young monk read dreadfully.

He kept stumbling and pausing quite incongruously. His voice was like a child's in a village school. The hallucinating, hysterical saint's tragic life made no impact on the minds of the monks. They must have heard it so often they had become inured. The monks ate hungrily; more than one really gorged. The fare was simple and frugal. The clash of forks on china plates was audible above the loathsome, jarring reading.

At the end of the meal, more prayers and solemn bowing.

Afterwards a procession forms and leaves the refectory singing the *Miserere*, and walks to Saint Dominic's tomb, where it disperses after they have said a prayer. Work begins in the monastery.

I wandered along a gallery with windows that look towards distant mountains, grey massifs with pools of glinting silver, and bumped into the monk from that strange encounter in the organ loft.

I approached him and we chatted. Conversed about music. 'Do you like music a lot?' I asked, and he smiled pleasantly and replied, 'More than you can ever imagine, but I was forced to abandon it because it was making me coarse. It is lasciviousness itself … I'll give you a piece of advice … abandon music if you don't want to live a life of torment. Everything about it rings false … Now my only music is Gregorian plainchant …'

Then we chatted about other things. The monk is a man of deep emotions and exceptional wisdom. 'One can see,' I said, 'you were once a man of the world.' 'Too much so!' he exclaimed sadly. 'But I, who suffered so much when I lived in the world of men, have found this place to be a haven of peace and serenity. I am growing old and harbour no illusions, this is where I want to die …'

He told me he was the closest friend of the brilliant Darío Regoyos and that the people who visit him in the monastery include Zuloaga and Unamuno … a glass shelf displays some of the paper birds the great thinker from Salamanca makes in his spare time. This Benedictine artist is undoubtedly a wonderful man.

We go our different ways. He has to study, because he will soon lead the singing of mass. His figure vanishes into the back of the gallery to the silky rustle of his robes.

The only noise comes from the fountain in the Romanesque courtyard and the chirping of birds above the trees in the garden.

A time for private, meditative sadness.

Shadows

The distant cloak of night draws near.

The mountains sink into streaks of light on the horizon
... A blue haze wraps itself around the monastery.

When we leave the refectory after dinner we walk to the
kitchen garden. The monks have a moment for recreation.
The garden gleams mysteriously at twilight. Everything is
quiet and monastic ...

Old monks stroll along the paths between fruit-trees
arguing about theology and holy matters, novices laugh and
play on a hillock among the branches of trees. Frogs croak
in ponds and water-runs; meanwhile a full moon visits the
august calm peering between the mountains, its divine light
floods the precinct, beautiful and magnificent, aristocratic
and patriarchal. Dogs bark.

Two aged monks bow their heads and stand anxiously in
a corner of the garden by a pond full of moss and weed where
the moon contemplates itself in the rippling water.

A lizard hides in the long grass.

It is twilight's final hour and the shadows of temptation
anticipate making an appearance ... The old men bend down
and pray quietly, hopelessly; the young men fight till they
vanquish or don't ... Beyond the mountains, and beyond
that beyond, begins the blood-stained interrogation of the
infinite ... The bronze bell chimes wearily summoning them
to dark prayers of supplication.

The kitchen garden is deserted.

The living shade of Gonzalo de Berceo traverses rustling branches, sighs and brandishes his broken lute ... The last glimmer of light has gone, and the wind from the sierras soon begins to spread their scented beauty ...

The monks pray in church without organ accompaniment. Dark shadows descend on all sides.

A yellowish light shines at the back of the temple, coalesces into a heart of fire. Amid the fearful pauses in their prayers, someone coughs.

When they conclude the *Magnificat* they have said flatly but with feeling, the abbot advances into the dark church and, praying devoutly, hyssop in hand, scatters holy water over the temple's shadowy depths.

I seem to hear a strange noise, as if someone were running. Evil demons rush to hide in their lairs, fleeing prayer and holy water. The shivering light illumines a red face ...

Nocturnal silence envelops the monastery ... The moon etches the columns on the cloister floors. The cypress is silhouetted over the roof. Once again I hear muffled steps and sounds of rosaries in the passageways. The fountain is quiet ... Only the moon filters into the entire monastery between the capricious shapes of the shadows ...

TOMBS IN BURGOS

❖ ❖ ❖ ❖ ❖

Embellishment

Embellishment constitutes the apparel and ideas that surround all artistic works. The general idea of a work is expressed in its lines. The first thing an artist must consider if he wants his soul to be better understood is the initial impact of his work on the eye, that is the creation in its entirety; however, to express his thoughts and philosophical intentions, he uses embellishment, and that is what speaks graphically and spiritually to the observer ... He must always take his themes into account, their tragic or emotional modulation that has to move most people, enigmatic figures that say all or nothing, lack of comprehension of which stimulates thought ... Then milieu, because everything must be in its proper place, and its influence is such that it changes his expression completely ... Time, the great destroyer and creator of illusions, is the supreme artist of melancholia. We feel times past in all their grandeur through monuments, in their history and colour ... and it seems ancient sculptors made their tombs to be looked at now ... And they hide such bitterness beneath the eternal evening colour of the cloisters ... They all elaborate the same sardonically packaged ideas of life and death ... as if eager to say things, things they couldn't say for fear of being burnt alive or shut up forever in a dingy prison.

As a general rule, the artists who created them, the same people who worked on the choir-stalls and in all the toil involved in making cathedrals, were ordinary folk and, as such, oppressed by the nobility and clergy ... When their calloused hands took up pencil and brush they did so with all the rage and perversity they could muster against those who enslaved them. Evidence of this can be found in the misericords in the stalls and the ideas behind the tombs ... Even the literature of the time sketches out their anticlerical ideas in symbolic figures that are difficult to interpret ... so many things are left unexplained! The artist placed two gentle-headed Jesuses as supports for a massive tomb where a bishop of old lies in peace; their weary faces sustain a heavy arch draped by a vine sagging under huge bunches of grapes ... This is very peculiar: it is well known that the saints, even when they acted as columns, never did so as caryatids, because the creators of façades took pity on them ...

The embellishment of ideas in Gothic tombs courses through the rich veins of vines where birds, snails and lizards twist and turn, fight with pelicans, nightmarish chimera and winged monsters with lions' heads. All very tiny as if they are afraid to be seen ... or as if that fauna engendered by the devil had hidden away among the bunches of grapes in flight from incense or funereal Gregorian chants ... The knight is always holding a book and is protected by angels and saints with a page or a dog at his feet ... Gothic flora blossom over the arches climaxing in clusters and bouquets. All Gothic artists took particular care not to disrupt lines and to give an impression of decorative simplicity; they injected their main philosophy and mockery into their figures.

If we stop by a Gothic tomb, we can observe the streams of grotesque little people, tiny demons studding the canopy fretwork like precious stones, very gentle shapes hiding in the shadows from the ashlars, but everything is there in seed form ... A style had to emerge to open these rich veins and allow them to spread over altarpieces and columns, and gave rise to a form that is inebriated by embellishment. The Baroque.

Gothic artists, in my view, are more incisive when depicting vices on their tombs. You find the cardinal sins portrayed there ... and on the occasional sepulchre the occasional sin is victorious ...

Then, naïve Stations of the Cross, scenes from sacred history and clusters of angels ... They placed the apostles on pillars alongside perversion, their faces ecstatic, enraged, serene ...

None the less, these tombs are more Christian and less pagan ... They are like a sampler of that era of great starvation and superstition ... full of terror of Beelzebub and picaresque, scheming wit. They are also a sampler of horrors that are now past, showing a thousand coats-of-arms and the wealth of a man who is now not even dust ...

Renaissance plaque, Burgos Cathedral

But you can feel a tremendous Christian faith dawning in Romanesque tombs; in the Renaissance all that Romanesque austerity and Gothic philosophy turn into pagan licentiousness kneaded with a peculiar mysticism that puts the soul in a quandary ... And elegant refinement yields to the strong classical lines of the Romans and Greeks ... Plinths with apples, roses and cornucopias triumph and garlands of skulls tied with silver ribbons, and satyrs struggling with huge leaves and friezes of an assortment of heads, which the pilgrim Santiago prods with his staff ...

The ideas are incomprehensibly curious ... As a general rule these Renaissance tombs, like most Gothic ones, take the form of altars: it is the form that best lends itself to a wealth of embellishment ... Every line frames a tableau brimming with figures and flowers.

On some plinths naked women swathed in scarves and garlands of oranges seem to be suffering greatly as they support baskets of ivy, in others caryatids melt into the wall, their hair, dishevelled by an icy wind, supports the entire fabric of the tomb ... all bearing broken bulls and lions' heads, the teeth of which grasp the bows linking garlands that are running riot.

In some the nudes are drawn in all their frenzied lust, in others their brazen spirit contains a silent sadness that transcends religiosity ... An old abbot rests in that funeral urn supported by two stark naked men openly displaying their sexual parts, though their movements and half-closed eyes are imbued with the grandeur of infinite purity ... and their expressions are soft and gentle while other tombs have faces and beautifully writhing bodies that are lasciviousness itself ...

And they filled unadorned spaces with dragons, dragons with exquisite faces and well-drawn features, women with eagles' talons and open wings in a tumult of leaves and horns, and rams with glaring eyes, soothsaying birds entangled in roses with hundreds of leaves, ogres, grieving bacchantes, thistles, acanthus, a whole symphony of tempting illusions crowned by the majestic scene from Calvary, sustained by pyramids of branches or the shoulders of a colossus ...

In late Renaissance tombs sumptuous nudity gives way to marvellous sheaves of lines and coats-of-arms as the only source of embellishment ...

✥ ✥ ✥ ✥ ✥

In its entire history of sorrowing, humanity seems to possess a great desire to perpetuate lives, or rather, lives that want to speak to us eternally through stones and funeral arches ... A tomb always questions ...

Man's vanity contains a black inner void that prevents him from seeing the great beyond. Vanity is always in the present. A man thus besotted can never understand that the memory of himself and the good or bad things he did will fade, and when he thinks of perpetuating his memory, he thinks he will witness all the possible homages that may be paid to him ... or at least imagines that to be the case ...

It is dispiriting to visit cloisters full of dusty, yellow-green tombs from which time has erased the names ... What were these people thinking when they ordered such ornate tombs to be built? Nobody looks upon them with the superstitious respect they hoped to inspire. They are simply there and will surely be moved to a place where archaeologists can study them at their leisure ... Time is the slayer of all vanity, and however loudly they clamoured or wanted to endure, the shackles of silence will respond as sarcastically as the sea that parodied the cries of Prometheus ...

Vanity is certainly the ugliest of passions and locks all stupid men in its ark ... The vain man is puerile and offensive to everyone ... He takes up residence within us and we can never rob him of his desire for pleasure and the past ... but the latter and the heart's tremendous passions are astonishingly beautiful. And we all feel similarly because the figure of Venus naked against a backcloth of foam and blue tritons is embedded in our brains ... And nobody, absolutely nobody will ever unleash himself from sins that bring so much bitter sweetness ... because we are made of such stuff ... but after death there is a proper place for everything *except* vanity. And we think of these lords preparing their tombs in their youth, being sculpted out of marble and rock and hoping that people would look at them in awe like our beloved Cervantes in Seville Cathedral ...

The vainglorious did not survive from the past generations of funereal Egypt, now all truncated and reduced to smithereens ... And their desire for immortality was so great that they fled from mounds that were more easily destroyed and placed their tombs on walls like altars. As in Gothic funereal architecture ... The funereal always provokes thought and fills the soul with emptiness ... When we gaze at a sepulchre, we intuit the corpse within, without gums, a mass of creepy-crawlies like Becerra's mummy, or smiling satanically like Valdés Leal's bishop ... And these thoughts become entangled in the fatuous branches and bouquets that cover the urn, and terror in the presence of death that belongs to Rubens ... when we contemplate these stony chests of putrefaction, the horrendous horsemen of the Apocalypse according to Saint John the Divine appear in the distance ... Churches sin when they allow vanity to enter their naves ... Jesus Christ said man must return to the earth from which he came, or should be laid in the fields to be fodder for crows and scavengers, as in the old traditions of India ... A corpse must never be preserved because it is bereft of devotion and faith, quite the contrary ... and the corpses of saints must be the first to pay their fleshly tribute to the earth, like the ancient patriarchs, because that is the way to give death its supreme serenity and mystery ... That's why the reliquaries containing the bones of virgins and tormented ascetics who saw Satan in the guise of a thousand naked bodies, who plucked their hearts out in a lunatic quest for the ideal, should be scattered over the fields where they were born. And should never harangue men about what they ought to be because that is what they will become, and that *is* the lesson they must teach, and if you want to adore a man, adore his spirit in your memory, never produce a tibia of his wrapped in withered flowers and glass ... Flesh rules life; let the soul live on in death ... But time is a tragic demon! No one inhabits most of the tombs I contemplate. Those who

Gothic Capital, Burgos Cathedral

slept here and hoped to see the light were scattered over fields when the people had an attack of madness ... A skull still exists in some, a bone like a lump of coal or lead, and spiders, great friends of darkness and silence ... and we no longer think that mound or altar before us is a tomb; once the body was gone, it lost its funereal aura. Then do we give form to the spirit of things ...? Or is the body a tomb ...?

Naturally, once an urn is shattered, it loses all its sad charm and mystery, because its origin and *raison d'être* have gone and everything else is quite secondary from the point of view of first impressions …

That is why tombs of men who have recently died are so fearful of the midnight hour and that morbid delight in wanting, yet not wanting, to lift the lid and contemplate, yet not contemplate, the horror of putrefaction …

The presence of the dead is more palpable in the solemnity of a Romanesque tomb than on supine Gothic altarpieces, and what most chases the dismal idea of death from the mind is a vigorous recumbent statue like those sculpted by Fancelli and El Borgoñón … or the statues of the monarchs of Castile, Juan I and his wife placed on a Gothic façade surrounded by apostles and virtues … I have found the most powerful ideas suggestive of corpses on tombs in the enclosed convent of Santa María de las Huelgas, veritable catafalques redolent with medieval severity, protected by an old writhing, screaming Christ … And you cannot imagine a king entered there with pomp, ceremony and ululations, nor think the valour of Alfonso VIII has transmuted into a black stone pigsty swamped by sheets of simple-minded petitions invoking his spirit … That is why the idea of a sepulchre is tantamount to a fainting swoon in terms of the future … Almost all these tombs in Burgos that enclose so many magnificent ideas … are empty … and all there is now is a heap of sardonic inscriptions on dull-coloured parchments that speak solemnly about indulgences and the glories of the dead who no longer exist even as ashes … and you feel strange contemplating La Cartuja's empty sepulchres where an amphora contained the entrails of Philip the Fair, in front of which Joanna the Mad passionately cried her heart out before the body housing his soul, as did Brunilda before Siegfried in the epic *Nibelunglied* ... That is why the coldness of spirit with which you contemplate tombs devoid of corpses meets coldness from the past as you tell the beads of an impossible rosary of a remote ideal ... Today all that has flown those carved stone piles that enclose a bone or stifling darkness ... When we contemplate the thoughts that inspired them, we simply see visions of those far-off times and re-discover lost illusions ... and can only think of human vanity that has been so punished and mocked by centuries of levelling ... and, in particular, we think how all this must come to an end ... because the world and eternity are also but an infinite dream ...

LOST CITY

✤ ✤ ✤ ✤ ✤

Baeza

For Señorita María del Reposo Urquía

Everything is vaguely soporific ... as if ancient shadows walk the sad, silent streets that will weep at midnight ... Everywhere are ruins the colour of blood, arches transformed into arms that want to embrace, broken columns covered in yellow and ivy, heads melting into damp earth, coats of arms fading into green darkness, verdigris crucifixes that speak of death ... Then a sweet sound of bells echoes continuously in the inner ear ... children's voices ring out in the distance and incessant barking drowns out everything ... The brightest light and bluest sky sharply silhouette palaces and ramshackle houses ablaze with oriflammes of hedge-mustard. No one walks these streets, and if someone does, he does so very slowly as if afraid of arousing light sleepers ... Weeds rule the streets and spread through the city concealing roadways, framing houses and removing

Lane behind the Cathedral, Baeza

any trace of passers-by. Cypresses bring melancholy to the scene like huge censers perfuming the air in a city constantly dissolving into red dust ...

There are flaking façades with mouldering, grotesque, terrified faces, broken pediments that are dripping with damp ... columns embedded in walls that seem to be writhing and trying to break free from their prison ... All is quiet. Silent.

At night the sound of steps disappearing into the dark ... one after another, after another ... and the breeze whispers on street-corners ... and the moon beams down molten silver ... Patios are stocked with tulips, boxwood, larkspur, lilies, nettles and moss ... There are scents of camomile, round-leafed mint, hay, roses, crumbling rock, water and sky ... Even the most cherished objects wear the tragic stamp of neglect.

Roofs, balconies and lintels are adorned with topaz, garnet and mossy emeralds. Poplars and ring-doves break the grey monotony ...

The dark streets are romantic, blue-lit passages, with soot-black Christs and anguished Virgins, cobwebbed street-lights that are never switched on.

All ruled by the cathedral's black, solemn harmony.

Grey-brown towers and smoky stairs leading nowhere in particular, ruined battlements that are nests of insects and shadows that hide when someone walks by.

Now and then remarkable Renaissance palaces and mansions adorned with statues and lovely rose windows ...

After walking under arches and down fortified lanes, you happen upon a dismal slope overgrown with brambles and acacias that acts as anteroom to the city's tired, melancholy heart. It is always solitary and deeply sad, traversed only by canons strolling to their prayers and birds flying wildly hither and thither, unsure where to settle.

Weeds are almost engulfing alive a triangular house on one side of this square and other down-at-heel edifices with doors almost unhinged by tedium. The ground is greeny velvet. An austerely pagan fountain stands in the centre with the last figure from a triumphal arch the earth must have swallowed up.

The overbearing cathedral perfumes the square with incense and wax that filter through its walls as a reminder of its sanctity.

In the distance, houses of golden stone with age-old inscriptions commemorating heroic deeds faded by too much sun, and windows flaking behind rusty, rickety grilles.

The square is painfully, privately silent ...

The palace of the old Town Hall on one corner is a black, green and yellow pile and very dull. Its windows stare vacantly out amid shadowy half-erased coats of arms.

Crosses and hedge-mustard hang down like votive lamps, and red flowers squeeze between cracks and stripe the entire façade.

Cathedral bells fill these spaces with sweet, metallic peals in a lordly melody the other city bells accompany with gently mournful timbres.

When I visited Baeza, they were planning to profane this square, this dramatic expression of the Romantic where the antique reveals its melancholy lineage, a place of rest,

Plaza de la Cruz Verde, Baeza

peace and virile sadness. The mayor had proposed it should be urbanised (dreadful, obscene word), the hallowed weeds uprooted and the fountain surrounded by little English gardens; they probably hope to erect a monument there to Don Julio Burell or Don Procopio Pérez y Pérez and perhaps one day this mysterious, mournful square will house a ghastly bandstand and a band strike up *pasodobles* and *cuplés* by Martínez Abades, and *habaneras* by Maestro Nieto. They will demolish this delightful old spot and put in its place buildings made from Catalan cement. What is happening in Spain to architectural relics is most distressing … Everything is being turned topsy-turvy … by the most deplorable artistic vision.

S Juan Evangelista, Baeza

Let us recall the great square in Santiago de Compostela and its monument to Señor Montero. What a hateful gob of spit on the wondrous Churrigueresque façade of the Obradoiro and the imposing hospital! Let us recall the disfiguring of Salamanca, the Palace of Monterrey lined with electricity posts, the House of Death and its fractured balconies, La Salina converted into a local government office, and likewise in Zamora, Granada and León ... Local political bosses have a mania for demolishing ancient things and replacing them with monuments orchestrated by Benlliure or Lampérez ...! And we Spaniards are so pitiful we simply walk on, heartless and unaware...! The new dawn of love and peace will never come while we fail to respect beauty and ridicule those that beauty inspires with passionate sighs ...! Wretched, illiterate country where to be a poet is the height of absurdity ...!

If you take a few steps, you descend into a well of softly moving shadows and espy an aged saint who died on a quiet mule ride from Granada, now embedded in the wall above a squat *mudéjar** door and a cathedral archway ...

A weary, exhausted figure emerges at a Byzantine pace from moonlit stonework where the hedge-mustard plays games with the shadows. This gate is called the Moon's because the moon alone bathes it in mystical light ...

If you walk further on, the clumps of grass are so thick

Mudéjar: the term used to describe art and architecture created by Muslims working in areas that had become Christian again from the beginning of the fall of the Peninsular Arab kingdoms in the twelfth century to the Christian capture of Granada in 1492.

they engulf the stones and anxiously lick the walls ... and if you cross a few more alleyways, a majestic symphonic landscape comes into view: a huge glen surrounded by blue mountains where diamantine white villages sparkle through the murky light. The dark wild chords of olive groves contrast with the deep purple foothills of the sierra. The Guadalquivir traces a huge squiggle over the plain. The earth undulates gently but energetically ... The cornfields shiver, gripped by the winds. The city skulks on the slope in flight from the solemn bravura of the landscape.

But a sense of sadness and nostalgia predominates ... The air is so cool and intensely perfumed ... Carts clatter and grumble past in the distance stirring up clouds of dust ...

There are occasional sudden blazes of red flowers on the eaves of some of the houses.

Only the sun strolls the steep streets against an indigo, silver-clouded sky.

This mute city is home to remnants of cemeteries with one-eyed, crumbling crosses and façades silenced by so much talk of dead things ...The water-channels flatten grass that trembles in the breeze.

Some streets seem really Andalusian with whitewashed houses and windows jutting out under the eaves ... then disappearing into a backcloth of dazzlingly luminous country-side ... The silence and tranquillity are what disturb most in these outlying streets ... The only sounds are of a child crying, doors creaking or the gentle harmonies of the breeze and the sun.

A girls' choir is singing a very bad version of a tender lyric

doorway, Baeza

forged in melancholy Schubert's crucible in a quiet square that sports an elegant if flaking little palace, a pretty little altar with rag flowers next to a haughty triumphal arch with a bellicose air and a fountain where lions are sketched on stone:

Star over the meadow
Come out to the country
And pick the flowers
Of May and April ...

A children's song with a pleasant, moving lilt ... a deeply poetic song, particularly when it rings out on a moonlit summer's night in a village.

When we revisit these streets, we always discover something of interest ... a capriciously designed capital embedded in a wall, a grille made for a lover's serenade, a whitewashed palace that's been destroyed ... though everything is neglected and scorned ... and anything that *has* been refurbished bears the stamp of the profaners of art.

Dusk seen from these heights is musical and tranquil ... On the splendid horizon blue amber clouds ... conceal the light of a glass strawberry of a sun.

A tremolo of moon and stars is a prelude to nightfall.

✤ ✤ ✤ ✤ ✤

Infinite melancholy of ancient stones coated in verdigris and gold!

The great sorrow of graveyard streets where no one walks! Splendidly inebriated on romanticism!

Swallows swoop through the air embroidering the silvery light ... The interior of the cathedral seems illuminated by red lamplight.

The hearts of would-be dreamers are downcast or expand in search of warm air or a generous ideal ...

Seeking refuge in these old cities, worldly, disconsolate souls find an atmosphere of sad resilience ... and emotional conflict is exacerbated ... with such different meanings.

When we walk through their recondite, dreamy shadows,

feeling alone, our hearts anxious, sorrow resolves our doubts, but we are more spiritually at peace. We occasionally descend into an enviable nirvana, and our bodies are like the stones of these ancient palaces that sleep the dream of eternity; at others we laugh optimistically or else grey blood wells in our hearts ... but among stones of gold we are always intoxicated by romanticism.

A Proclamation in the Afternoon

A time for luxuriating in the month of June. An empty street. Houses of gold with unintelligible inscriptions to heroes are as strong and silent as a convent. The street is a mass of weeds. White-branched acacias huddle next to noble mansions, hide under their balconies away from the sun's fire. Sometimes their plumes sway in anguish as if protesting against their oppressor. The light on a church façade is blinding when it hits the stones.

The proclamation rang out in the distance. It was a sorrowful cry of anguish, like a lamentation by someone who complains in artistic vein ... Proclamations can be amusing, appealing and fill the space where they resound with joy. They are short choruses, city refrains. The same proclamations in Granada are full of melancholy cheer ... but the one that echoed through Baeza at three on a June afternoon was simply mournful.

The town-crier's voice bawled out.

There was silence and it resounded again.

Such proclamations are usually one or two notes repeated rhythmically in a single key, particularly when proclaimed by Andalusian town-criers ... but this cry echoed through the forgotten city like a Wagnerian chorus. First a plaintive, weary refrain that vibrated like a bell chiming in a major key, then repeated as an *andante maestoso*, followed by a pause. Then the same theme was repeated, now quietly, before the voice took on a guttural strain, slipped into minor key, reached a high pitch, then dipped languidly back on the opening note. The proclamation echoed, faded, echoed, like a phrase played on the great Wagner's horn ...

The figure of the person singing appeared at the end of the gently sloping street.

She was a barefoot, bent old hag, her dank, grey hair trailing down her back, bleary-eyed, head bowed, as if immersed in deepest meditation. She carried a basket full of rabbit skins, old utensils and useless rags ... She repeated the proclamation three times as she walked down the sunny street. Her strange, iron rhythms made you want to flee her tune as if it were a curse.

There were interludes of silence when the town-crier disappeared from sight. Finally, her voice faded and the street was empty and bored by the intense heat ...

The acacias barely stirred.

CHRISTS

❖ ❖ ❖ ❖ ❖

There is a devotion that surpasses all others in the soul of the people: devotion to the man crucified.

From the remotest times dead Jesus's drooping head has terrified simple folk. But this devotion and fearful piety was and is felt by the people today as a tragic reality, not for its spiritual grandeur. That is, they fear and pity Christ because of the terrible pain searing his body, not because of the boundless sea of his soul, and are horrified by his bruises and bleeding sores, and weep over his crowns of thorns but never meditate on and love the spirit of God that suffers in order to bring ultimate consolation.

In all representations of Christ on the cross, artists exaggerated the blows from sticks and lances, the horrifically contracted muscles ... and thus communicated the man's suffering to the people, as the only way of bringing the great drama to the multitude ... And the unlettered multitude looked and learned but saw only the external ... Artists failed to portray God on a single Calvary, but only portrayed the man, and some, like the renowned German, Matthias

Grünewald, painted the most frightening passion of Jesus and did so by creating a man who is too much of a man, where the death of God is nowhere to be seen.

Nobody can interpret God defeated yet glorious, because no human brain can encompass such an immense concept ... and that is why all Christs are the man crucified, with the expression anyone would display dying from such savage torture ... Sculptors of old conceived their ancient Christs as rigid, with huge heads and crude faces, wild and iron-hard as the epic times in which they lived ... always taking care to emphasise the crown of thorns, the sores on the ribs or the writhing belly, so that their work conveyed all the horror to the people ... anguished stance, contorted fingers, eyes bulging out of their sockets in pain... People needed the scene on Calvary to give their faith deeper roots ... They could feel Jesus on the cross when they saw his sublime head split open, his chest heaving, his heart on the ground, the blood foaming from his mouth, and they wept to see him precisely in that place where he suffered least, because by now the end was in sight, he was God on the cross and his astounding sacrifice was fact ... but when the people thought of Jesus crucified they never remembered Jesus in the Garden of Gethsemane, only their pain and fear at the sight that shocked them, nor were they astonished by Jesus's human love at the Last Supper ...

Tragedy, what is real, speaks to people's hearts and that is why artists who sought widespread fame always created a Christ full of purple pustules, and speaking in this manner they were understood ... Then came the primitives with their cold

Christs, and Romanesque sculptors with their stiff effigies ... and sculptors and painters who gave a sense of reality ... They created those black Christs we see carefully put to one side, then chose to give them long hair and colour, began to give movement to the lines and finally the impression that they were human ... And it was Spanish colourists who so closely observed his agony and created a crucified man, a bruised and battered body in all its spine-chilling reality.

Energetic sturdy Christs, glistening white, without sores, nailed to the cross as if they could be anywhere at all, that the artist only depicted with the frigid nudity of a tailor's dummy, are never the object of popular devotion ... Perfection never generates flights of passion; what disturbs and anguishes the masses is the expression ... The appalling tragedy people see in some crucifixions is what induces their love for them ... but they have little grasp of God's feeling, the grandiose disconcerts and terrifies ... The men who made those Christs we find hidden away in dark chapels lit by reddish light, brawny arms twisted on the cross, heads concealed by a cascade of burnt hair, surrounded by old dusty ex-votos, those fearful, smoky Christs were made by inspired artists who thought profoundly. They understood the people. They are extremely poor artistically, the dimensions are peculiar, the execution ludicrous, the hair quite improbable, but they give a terrible sense of the horror and so are loved by the masses ... This is one of the many proofs that art is not simply refined technique but needs the giant, mysterious flame of inspiration if it is to speak out ... And much more so in the art of religious sculpture where the artist should only be concerned to make the mainly uncultured multitude think and feel ... because understanding other arts requires a special, spiritual education ... And these creators of old Christs who, it is often said, are poorly made, knew how to instil fear into the soul ...

The people had an instinctive feel for artistic genius and wove endless legends and fables around these images ... and garlanded them in cloth roses and covered them in crutches, eyes and locks of hair and placed skulls and serpents at the foot of the cross, where the people prayed, prayed in terror, before that appalling love of man. These swooning Christs are generally tucked away in small village chapels where they are the pride of the local inhabitants ... The brilliant sculptors of Spain who were more thoughtful and interested in ideas emerged later and they made their Calvaries by putting their soul into the creation of Christ's eyes. Mora, Hernández, Juni and El Montañés, and Salzillo, and Siloé, and Mena and Roldán, etc., etc. knew how to infuse Jesus's eyes with dramatic gentleness ... and made them half-closed and blood-curdling like Mora's, or convulsed and looking glassily at the ground like Mena's, or staring into the sky beseeching eternity like El Montañés's, or hanging out of their sockets, greenish and moribund like Siloé's Christ in La Cartuja ... These sculptors realised a contorted body says a lot, and eyes in agony say much more ... and put all the suffering racking that idealised body into the eyes ... But all crucifixions invoke surrender to the irrevocable expressed by the way the head droops, suffused with the invisible twilight pallor death brings, death that is always mystical ...

GRANADA

✤ ✤ ✤ ✤ ✤

Summer Dawn

The distant mountains surge and ripple lazily like a serpent. An infinitely crystalline translucency reveals matt splendour on all sides. Night spills shadows over green arbours and the city languidly sheds its veils to display its domes and ancient towers in the soft golden light.

Empty-eyed houses peer out of the foliage and grass; poppies and vines dance cheerfully to the sound of a sunny breeze.

Shadows lift lethargically and fade as shrill birds pipe on their ocarinas and reed flutes.

In the distance there are hesitant mists and heliotropes of poplars, and in the cool of morning a distant bleat occasionally hits the key of F.

Black and white wood pigeons fly down the blue and green Darro valley and settle on poplars or clumps of yellow flowers.

dawn in the gardens of the Alhambra

The bass bells are still slumbering, and only the occasional Albaicín sheep's bell tinkles ingenuously next to a cypress.

Bulrushes, reeds and wild herbs bend over the water and kiss the sun when they see themselves reflected there ...

The sun seems almost not to shine ... and the moment the shadows lift ... a pale purple tinges the city, the mountains turn to solid gold and the trees gleam in an Italianate apotheosis.

The hazy, pastel blue tones transmute into splendid bursts of light and the ancient towers of the Alhambra are luminously red morning stars ... the whitewash of the houses scorches and the groves are the brightest green.

The Andalusian sun begins to sing its song of fire that all things dread to hear.

The light is so marvellous and unique that the birds flying though the air seem fashioned from rare metals, massive irises and pink opals ...

Smoke starts to rise from the city, covering it in heavy incense ... The sun shines and the sky, once pure and fresh, turns a dirty white. A mill strikes up its sleepy serenade ... A nostalgic rooster sings of the red dawn and cicadas in the Vega frenziedly tune their violins in anticipation of a drunken noon.*

*The Vega of Granada is the fertile valley beyond the city that was cultivated by the Romans and later the Arabs, until their expulsion in 1492 by Ferdinand and Isabel.

Albaicín

For Lorenzo Martínez Fuset, a fine friend and companion

The white houses rise up the hillside to ghostly echoes … The Alhambra's golden towers opposite are silhouetted against the sky in an oriental fantasy.

The Darro issues ancient lamentations and splashes against vistas from Moorish tales. The sound of the city vibrates in the air.

The Albaicín's towers soar full of *mudéjar* gracefulness … There is infinite harmony outside. Hovels dance gently around the hill. Bitter, dark green shapes of prickly pears stand out from time to time against the white and red of the houses … Churches tower over convent belfries that cloister their bells behind latticed shutters and peal in divine early morning Granada, responding to the honeyed Watch Tower.

On splendidly bright days in this magnificent city, the Albaicín stands out against the sky's distinct blue and brims with rural grace.

The dramatic streets are narrow and curious, lop-sided stairs, sinuous tentacles twisting capriciously and wearily to small vantage points with views of huge snowy mountains or the Vega's magnificent harmonies. Some streets are scary, disturbing paths formed by walls cloaked in jasmine, creepers and Saint Francis roses. Dogs bark and distant voices call out, sensual and disappointed. Others spiral down inclines that are impossible to descend, littered with boulders, walls gnawed by time, where tragic women, reduced to an idiot state, sit and look provocative ...

The houses cluster curiously as if blown together by a hurricane. They huddle in zany, vertical patterns, lean into each other, walls clashing in a startling devilish snarl. Apart from the way *granadinos* (who don't deserve the name)

the Alhambra & the Albaicín, Granada

have mutilated some features, this dreamy neighbourhood remains distinctive ... As we wander along its byways, scenes from romantic tales suddenly come into view.

Altars, wrought-iron grilles, huge, apparently uninhabited houses, timorous cisterns where the water possesses the tragic mysteries of a personal drama, crumbling entrance-ways where a fountain moans in the shadows, deep, rubbish-filled gullies under the small towers in the walls, streets trodden by no one, where doors are few and far between ... and then that

alley in the Albaicín, Granada

door is closed, abandoned hovels, red earthen slopes where petrified octopuses of agave gesticulate. The black caverns of nomads from the Orient.

Here and there the Moorish echoes of prickly pears ... And people in fearful, tense corners invent tales of dead bodies and wintry ghosts, of dwarfs and hobgoblins who come out at midnight, when no moon lights these paths, seen by errant midwives and prostitutes who gossip wildly, terrified and full of superstition. The Albaicín of fear and fantasy inhabits these crossroads, the Albaicín of barking dogs and grieving guitars, of dark nights on streets between whitewashed walls, the tragic Albaicín of superstition, of witches who read the cards and tell fortunes, of strange gypsy rites, of cabbalistic signs and amulets, of sorrowing souls, of pregnant women, the Albaicín of old prostitutes only too familiar with the evil eye, of seductresses, of horrible curses, of passion ...

In other corners of these ancient places, a truly romantic spirit of Granada seems to stir ... A deeply lyrical Albaicín ... Silent streets overgrown by weeds, beautiful façades, white minarets where the usual green and grey teats gleam, and colourful, sonorous gardens. Streets inhabited by people with an ancient turn of mind, whose sitting-rooms are adorned by large armchairs, hazy paintings and ingenuous urns with garlanded Baby Jesuses under arches of bright flowers, people who produce lamps with bygone shapes when the Eucharist passes and who own musty silks and shawls.

Streets of whitewashed, perpetually enclosed convents, with squat belfries and dusty latticed shutters reaching to the eaves ... where pigeons and swallows nest. Streets for sere-nading where nunnish virgins process ... Streets that hear the Darro's silvery melody and ballads of leaves sung by the Alhambra's distant woods ... A beautifully romantic, lordly Albaicín. An Albaicín with the Santa Isabel convent garden and entrances to secluded villas. An Albaicín of fountains, arbours, cypresses, flowering grilles, of a full moon and ancient ballads, an Albaicín of cornucopia, monkish organs, Arab patios, grand pianos, vast drawing rooms moistened by the smell of lavender, cashmere shawls and carnations ...

When walking these streets you sense the mystical is battling against the voluptuous. Numbed by the alarming succession of shadows and slopes, you glimpse the gentle colours of the silvery valley, melancholic and iridescent ... and the recumbent city dozing in the misty haze that severs at the neck the golden harmonies of a cathedral showing off its magnificent ambulatory and angel of victory tower.

These are tragic contrasts. On one empty street you hear the organ sweetly played in a convent ... and the divine greeting of *Ave María Stella* spoken by soft feminine voices. A man in a blue smock swears horrifically as he feeds his goats in front of the convent. Further on prostitutes, their big, jet-black eyes ringed in purple, shout horrendously coarse obscenities; next to them a delicate ragamuffin of a girl sings a pious song ...

All this creates an atmosphere of infinite distress: a curse from the Orient has descended upon these streets.

Air charged with twanging guitars and lazy gypsy cries.

Nuns' voices and the bustle and bite of flamenco.

The Vega and the city are as tranquil and majestic as this Moorish neighbourhood is anguished and tragic.

Reminders of the Arab past are everywhere. Soot-black arches, squat, paunchy houses with ornate galleries, mysterious hovels with oriental lines, women who have apparently just escaped from a harem ... A vagueness in the way people stare as if they dream of time past ... and crushing weariness.

If a woman calls out to her children or anyone, it is to make a languid complaint; drooping arms and unkempt hair give an impression of hostages to fortune and a truly Muslim belief in fate. Gypsy rhythms are always in the air, accompanied by despairing or mocking, deep-throated songs. You see golden hills and Arab walls. Transparent water flows from gashes in the rock, slips and curls down the street.

In kitchens, pots of carnations and geraniums eye saucepans and copper kettles, and open pantries in the damp earth are stuffed with Moorish crockery from Fajalauza.

Under the fierce sun scents rise, dampness, wax, incense, wine, rams, urine, dung and honeysuckle, and a strange din, dominated by the dark peals of the city's bells.

Exhaustion in sun and shade, eternal blasphemy and constant prayer. Chaste chimes summoning the choir are answered by guitars and drunken revelry from a bawdy house.

Funereal cypresses soar above houses in a display of romantic, sentimental darkness ... Close-by, the hearts and crosses of weathervanes turn gently against the majestic Vega.

A Nightmarish Canephora

Eyes a bilious yellow, a horrible figure in rags erupts from a cracked, peeling black door in a haze of damp green incense ... Behind her an ancient patio ... a moss-cobbled patio where perhaps eunuchs once slept in the moonlight, with Arab shadows on the walls and a deep, forbidding well ... Rickety balustrades support pots of faded geraniums and consumptive creepers embrace grimy columns ... Beyond that a pigsty and on a wall a dread Christ in a dance dress, decked in rag flowers ... An unappetising vomit of flies and a thousand wasps buzz menacingly. In the bluest sky, a fiery sun ... and out she staggered.

I don't know if my eyes saw right, or didn't even see her; the horrendous immediately bewilders our minds.

She cut a repulsive, mysterious figure.

No one was in the gloomy, lethally still street.

The monstrous figure didn't budge from the doorway. She had the cold, enigmatic allure of an Egyptian frieze.

Her belly was swollen as if eternally pregnant; her limp arms ended in viscous and phenomenally ugly hands. At her hip she carried a chipped pitcher and her thick greying hair framed a face with a gaping hole for a nose. Yellow scabs on her cheeks oozed stinking pus and a lurid eye shed tears over the pus wiped away by the grim figure's brawny hand ... She was departing that house of dread vices and lascivious extremes.

Sexually pungent and indecently attired, she might belong

to a rare species or be a Satanic hermaphrodite. Soulless flesh or Dantesque medusa. Fantasy by Goya or a vision seen by Saint John. Loved by Valdés Leal or torture for Jan Weenix … Her flesh was a deathly green. She coughed several times … and you thought you smelled sulphur … and felt the weight of evil spirits … The shocking apparition broke into a walk.

Her slippers hung half off and flopped lugubriously to her step; she wore dirty coral necklaces and a pouch around her neck that must have been an amulet from hell.

Inside, people laughed, clapped lustily and moaned in sorrow; a hoarse, boozy voice sang obscene ditties.

The monster dragged herself along like an lizard on two feet, and snarled either grinning or pained by life … She coughed again like a dog howling in a cellar and walked on, exuding a smell of rotten lavender and tobacco.

This beast in petticoats, her breasts sagging, is horrible to behold … She is the one always swearing in that house and scaring off good womenfolk. She would love to kiss us all and infect us with her disease. She is a female eunuch in a putrid harem. If she were beautiful, she would be Lucrezia; as she is horrid, she is Beelzebub. If she could choose a lover, it would be Neptune or Attila … if she could enact her curses, she would be like Hatto, the barbaric bishop of Andernach …

Such nightmarishly scary women sometimes stalk the Albaicín. They are the witches who catch passionate, black-eyed girls in their cabbalistic nets. They prepare beverages made from vipers, cinnamon and the bones of children crushed under a full moon. They keep good and evil spirits in their sewing-boxes ... and ignorant, superstitious mothers hang up golden horns and hallowed prints on their children to save them from their evil eye ...

But this nightmare ... How cold and withering is her way of walking down the sunny, rose-scented street! A sleep-stopping courtesan ...! Pitcher on hip, hands on ground, along the streets of the Albaicín ...

Sounds

For María Luisa Egea: so beautiful, magnificent and inspired ...
With all my devotion

From the towers of the Alhambra one can see the Albaicín and its patios with ancient galleries where nuns walk. *Via crucis* hang from whitewashed cloister walls. Cypresses languidly sway their scented, funereal mass next to romantically shuttered campaniles ... Patios of shadows and dreams ...

The convents bring an aura of sadness to the strong harmonies of the houses.

The midnight vision of the Albaicín from the fortress-cum-palace is a thing of mystery that attracts and fascinates ... And although the sight is strangely splendid and harbours powerful romantic voices, that isn't what fascinates. The sounds fascinate. You could say every single object has a sound ... that light, colour and shape make sounds.

In bursts of sound as intense as the mountains, woods

from a tower of the Alhambra

and plains, the landscape's musical range almost always has the same harmony that imbues other modulations. The foothills of the Sierra Nevada have delightful spaces of sound … Places imbued by the sound of the sweetly tempered scent of wild open country.

Amid the divine perfume from the pine woods, you can hear the gentle lilt of the grove, velveteen melodies even if a wind is blasting, gentle, warm, sustained modulations … always in the same key …

That is something Granada and its Vega don't possess when heard from the Alhambra. Each hour of the day has a different sound. You hear symphonies of sweet sounds … And unlike any other sonorous landscape I have ever heard, this romantic cityscape constantly changes pitch.

It has major and minor keys. It has passionate melodies and solemnly cold chords ... Sound changes with colour, so you can say that colour sings.

The sound from the Darro gives the scene harmony; it is a flute with a huge range of chords that each level plays differently. The breeze descends in a monotone, bringing scents from the sierra into the river gorge, handing on its sound to the streets of the Albaicín, where it quickly spreads bass and treble ... then over the Vega where it clashes against its wonderful sounds, distant mountains and clouds, creating a deep silver melodious lullaby that sends us all voluptuously to sleep ... On sunny mornings cheerful romantic music plays in the Darro's gorge. You could say the landscape sings in a major key ...

The bells peal in a thousand voices, and every one distinctive. The sonorous cathedral bells may chime in a tenor key, sending waves of music over the city ... They fall silent ... then, in magnificent counterpoint, receive responses from the Albaicín's various belfries. Bells chime frenziedly, spill out bronzed, passionate sound, melt into the whispering breeze, hiccup breathlessly ... Some virile peals fugue with distant vistas ... another, full of priestly unction, more tranquil and devout, issues a call to prayer that is at once weary and philosophically resigned ... The other bells that were pealing with passionate joy suddenly fall silent ... but the more tranquil bell continues reproachfully ... She is the old bell at prayer ... scolding the young ones for desires that will never become reality ... The bells that chimed with frantic enthusiasm until they died from their own sound were no

the Darro, Granada

doubt rung by mischievous acolytes in parish churches ... or by playful, shy novices in a convent, eager to laugh and to sing ... and almost certainly the bell now summoning us to prayer is rung by a grumpy old sacristan covered in candle-wax stains ... or a nun death has forgotten, who is in her convent awaiting the scythe's cut ... The silences are astonishing when the whole panorama bursts into song ... The cathedral bells chime again, the others gloss what their leader says ... and a childish, amusing cowbell refrain brings the symphony to a close ... its tinkling melody fades in a dying fall, as if refusing to end ... paring down to a final note that is almost inaudible. The symphonies played by the bells of Granada are wonderful and splendidly diverse!

Seen from this tower, the night is an array of wonderful, magical sounds. If moonlit, a vague, deeply sensual mood invades the chords, if there is no moon ... the river sings a unique, dreamy melody ... but it is twilight that generates the most original, intense variations where colour assumes the haziest of musical expressions. The ground has been prepared from mid-afternoon ... Shadows slip over the bonfire that is the Alhambra ... The Vega lies flat and silent. The sun hides and infinite waterfalls of musical colour burst from the hillsides and hasten soft and velvety over city and mountains, and the music of colour melds into the waves of sound ... invoking melody, ancient sadness and lamentation.

An irremediable, sorrowing grief spills over the houses in the Albaicín and the proud red-green slopes of the Alhambra and Generalife ... the colour changes continuously and with the colour, the sound. Pink, red, yellow sounds, imposs-ible sounds of colour and sound. Followed by a great blue harmony ... the night-time symphony of bells strikes up ... Almost all ring languidly, summoning us to the rosary ... The river erupts into song. Lights flicker in the Albaicín's narrow streets, making the black cypresses shiver in gold ... The Watch Tower begins its historic chant ... Tiny, timorous lights shine on bell-ringers in their chambers ...

A train whistles in the distance.

Summer Sunsets

When the sun slips behind pink-misted mountains and a colossal, contemplatively religious symphony suffuses the air, Granada is bathed in gold, pink and purple tulle.

Its corn wan and faded, the Vega dozes in a silvery yellow stupor, while far-off skies blaze in passionate violet and flames of sweetish ochre.

Wraiths of mist hover hesitantly above the ground like a smoke-saturated breeze, or hang heavily down like huge, solid silver nails. Heat and straw dust envelop the clusters of houses and the city drowns out the luxuriant greenery and sooty harmonies.

The foothills of the sierra are purple and dark blue and the peaks a pinkish white. Patches of snow spiritedly resist the fiery sun.

The rivers are almost dry and the water flows sluggishly along irrigation channels, as if transporting a deeply romantic

streetcorner in the Albaicín, Granada

soul exhausted after an evening of painful pleasures.

The moon's hieratic kiss pecks at the timidly blue sky above the sierra.

The sun's glare beats down on trees and vines ... and the blue, ashen green on the pink hills gradually cools and everything is bathed in the moon's hypnotic sheen.

When hardly any light is left, the city acquires a black veneer as if drawn from a single perspective, frogs begin their strange refrains and every tree seems to be a cypress ... The moon kisses everything, gently beams over the fretwork of branches, turns water to light, erases the loathsome, magnifies distances and transforms the Vega into a sea ... Then, an infinitely tender morning star, wind in the trees and the perennial, lulling sound of lapping water.

The night reveals its every charm under the moon. Dogs bark in the orchards overlooking the blue misty lake that is now the Vega ...

Winter Sunsets

The Vega is laid flat and the sad days of winter turn it into a succession of mirages.

Distant reaches veiled by fog are leaden grey and purple and the pallid poplar groves, thick, black stripes. The soft sky is white, flecked with black, light blue, a hazy delight. Houses glint and vanish in whitish smoke. The sound is muted like snow.

The initial boundaries are vigorously drawn. Silvery green olives cascade; tall, languid poplars weep; black cypresses sway gently. On the way out of the city pines bow their heads.

Every colour is pale and serious. Dark green and ruddy red dominate the foreground ... as they spread across the plain, the fog cloaks and erases them ... they become vague and dreamily distant. The rivers are huge incisions in the earth enabling the sky to see what is beneath.

In the course of hiding itself, the sun peered from the clouds ... and the Vega became an immense flower suddenly opening its great corolla in a wondrous display of its true colours. Huge consternation fills the landscape. The Vega shimmers magnificently. Everything shifts. Quick, lively colours spread out.

Deep blue tears stream down a nearby hillside ... There are hints of snow on the sierra beneath gauzy mists ...

Clouds accumulate, snap and snarl at each other, blacken ... and the rain falls fast and furiously. A dry, metallic sound of rain hitting lead pipes and guttering reverberates through the city ... A soft, springy noise of water on grass and water in the Vega ... The rain pitter-patters softly and splashes into pools and the sounds swoon when they hit the grass.

In the distance a thunderclap resounds like a monstrous drum ...

Frozen dead villages shrink ... paths are carpeted by large streaks of silver ... Rain pours menacingly down ... The light darkens; the haze deepens ...

Darkness and lethargy suffuse the Vega.

An intriguing white line gleams triumphantly on the horizon ... Beyond that, a mantle of black velvet studded with garnet stones covers the plain ...

GARDENS

✣ ✣ ✣ ✣ ✣

For Paquito Soriano, an admirable, exotic spirit

Our memories of gardens are the vaguest ... Melancholy overwhelms us when we walk through their shadowy arbours ... All melancholy is suffused with the scent from a garden ... The twilight hour makes gardens shiver in shades of colour that express the whole range of sadness ... Behind dark entangled ivy stirs the spirit of the woman pursuing us ... and between the quicksilver fountain and the constantly rustling leaves our fantasy creates spiritual visions from an inner world unleashed by the magic of those bowers. It is as if gardens were created to be reliquaries for every romantic scene that has taken place on earth. A garden is an exalted space, a summa of souls, silences and colours lying in wait to ambush mystic hearts and make them weep. A garden is a huge goblet overflowing with a thousand religious essences. A garden is an amorous embrace and an amphora of silent melancholia. A garden is a ciborium of passions and a grandiose cathedral for the most beautiful sins. Meekness, love and a vague sense of not knowing what step to take next lurk there ...

When they are a swathe of damp moss and no living shadows walk their paths, they are inhabited by sinuous dancers from the Orient who wend voluptuously between abandoned flowerbeds. When autumn comes, they are possessed by strange, profound mournfulness ...! One finds misty, forlorn gardens of consumptives who died in the verses of failed poets of old ...! Other gardens are full of *amour galant*, morbid statues, spume, swans, blue flowers, hidden libertinage, ponds with pink and green lotus flowers, languid storks and nude visions enclosing a whole life of sorrow and surrender to fate ... Gardens for oblivion and sensual souls ...! And some are a mass of green with black crannies where spiders have built their palaces of illusions ... where a cracked fountain bleeds, seeping through the rotten silk of algae ... Gardens for the idylls of nuns cloistered with a student or a tinker! Gardens that painfully recall a love that has vanished!

All spiritual figures that walk through a solitary garden do so slowly as if they are unconsciously performing a divine ritual ... and if they cross such a place at dusk or in the moonlight, they meld into its soul. All great meditations, ones that released something good and true, passed through a garden. The great individuals of romanticism mirrored gardens ... Music is a garden lit by a full moon. Spiritual lives are outpourings from a garden. Dreams! What are they if not our garden ...?

In the busy lives we lead, so full of trivial worries, few fear the subtle sorrows faced by a garden ... and the few who *are* born for a garden are swept along by the madding crowd. Romantics who sigh at the infinite elegance of a swan are almost no more ... At twilight gardens are alone. Evening's pinks and greys shroud them and rarely does anyone listen to their song.

A Convent Garden

Muted silence. Every colour is shy and chaste. Small daisies and wild flowers grow among untamed weeds ... Spiders have woven silvery threads over paths that nobody has trodden for years ... Occasionally damp humps of mossy green rise up like the back of a giant reptile ... The fountain is cracked and dry. Water trickles in one corner between dark grass and pale sunflowers, through dense weeds and disappears at the foot of the trees. The garden reflects the deep melancholy of the convent.

Nuns in grey-brown habits walk along the squat, impoverished galleries ... There is only one rose-bush in the whole precinct, tended by a novice who has not had time to become sad ... It is in a small recess in the cloister, next to a laurel tree. In the month of May its roses decorate the ingenuous Virgin.

The garden is so cold that everything withers ...

It instils beautiful, eternal calm despite the noise of shrill, nasal prayers and the sound from the wonderful organ … The convent has no bells … It is always autumn in this garden. Spring's vibrant gaiety and summer's sumptuous glare never enter here.

The shadowy bowers and oppressive stone sky mean the garden always lives the bitter melancholy of autumn. If there is one colour, it is a dull green, if there are flowers, they are yellow or faded blue … The cloister has no windows … The garden observes all the nuns' processions. There are no cypresses. The branches of the laurel tree twist their way inside through a window. The white sculpture of a holy father of the Church rots between the grass and the fence where water trickles: the nuns toppled it over because it served no purpose. The monstrous tower of the city's cathedral surges skywards, overlooks the garden, protects and dominates the convent. Strong creepers capriciously climb the patio walls … A nun tinkles a bell as she walks along cold, bare cloisters.

Gardens of Ruined Churches

You find humble, unkempt gardens on the way out from damp sacristies packed with dismantled altars, black chests and blurry mirrors.

They are almost always in ancient, weed-infested cemeteries, where a priest's housekeeper once planted rose-bushes and climbing plants. They are damp even though they receive sunlight. Reptiles live in crevices and crannies. A religious scent of incense wafts out from a broken church window. No one tends them, and, if they did, an ancient curse would fill them with nettles, hemlock, toadstools and other poisonous plants ... They are always large with dark stone walls overgrown by creeping tea roses, honeysuckle and ivy ... There are swarms of half-buried capitals and shady arches covered in ears of corn and poppies.

A broken fountain half-hidden by weeds rarely sings, when there is a surfeit of water in the city. Fig trees, camomile, fennel and morning glory prosper.

Some have gravestones with obliterated names stacked in a stinking corner; in others the sacristan's son looks after white doves and chained dogs that snarl; most have puddles of damp and walls wreathed by dandelion.

Almost invisible threads of silver on laurel trees, encrusted spurts of water ... and in corners no one visits, half-withered white rose-bushes.

These gloomy places usually hide walled-up ancient doorways behind trailing green plants and crumbling niches where worm-eaten saints wear winding-sheets of moss, plumes of grass and stiffly offer a blessing with contorted hands.

Some of these kitchen gardens lose their solemn character when creepers cover their walls ... but others are completely bare and still exhibit arches over niches and the occasional iron cross, rusted by time, languishing on the ground under the weeds.

In churches on the outskirts of towns, others are open to fields vibrant with colour ... Ivy and rose-bushes peer anxiously over many of these garden walls, then fall sweetly

... henbane, rue, poppies, lilies and devil's weed embrace between the stones ...

Sometimes the earth raises a flowerless void in the direction of strangely patterned stones, perhaps a remnant of a frieze that has disappeared and is placidly melting in the sun ... and all are ever so ... Rare is the garden that has fresh, luxuriant roses and pristine ponds with goldfish.

A Romantic Garden

Spanish gardens are disappearing. Tidy, symmetrical English parks are replacing them ... Only very infrequently, walking along a deserted path leading to humble places, do we come across a shadowy, deserted garden.

The romantic, gallant soul of the eighteenth century beats along its avenues. The garden loves pallid ladies and gentleman poets. Twilight gardens from an age of sentimental dramas. Misty gardens that made Juan Ramón Jiménez, the great poet of mists, suffer so ...

The garden was alone. Pink and white hollyhocks flourish their flowering staffs among green waves of myrtles that run riot. The green dome of a pergola overgrown by a tea rose rises in the centre of the garden. Inside dry leaves cover a black stone table. The benches have sunk into the wet ground and a cascade of ivy does its best to hide them ... Beyond that, a grimy Cupid on a crumbling pedestal fires his eternally lethal arrow, which is draped in creepers and spiders' webs ... There is a fountain in each corner of the garden. They are small and elegant; weed springs from their green-black bowls like the tresses of Gorgons that have drowned in the putrefied water ... They are almost invisible among the myrtles that, left untended, have grown spectacularly ... Water never splashes in this garden ... only at night do the irrigation channels sing in the distant fields. No birds visit this garden, except on moonless nights when the occasional mythical owl hoots from a shadowy lemon tree.

Next to the fountain in one corner, a statue of Apollo disintegrates, sheltering stiff with cold among rose-bushes ...

There is a veritable forest of cypresses. From a distance you would think it was an old cemetery ... Melodious and tragic, cypresses rise above flowerbeds and weaver's broom, along short, sad avenues ... The garden has even lost the legendary, lyric nightingale. It is so cold and there is such sadness in the air ...! Then there is the large house alongside the garden ... What deep sorrow in that façade with its windowless balconies where a poet might have sung at twilight, when they mirrored roses and cardamom! What bitterness in that abandoned mansion with its strange roof garden!

The balcony at one corner of the house is there as ever, the balcony that has been closed for years, the balcony still wept over by poets people describe as trite ... The piano is silent. Another moon spotlights the garden.

The poet notes the inner collapse. No white hands touch the keys; no doves settle on the shoulders of the eternal *Elle*; no ladders dangle from the balcony; no stormy loves in this garden ...

The poet runs his hands over his head and can feel how

he has lost his locks, sadly holds his hands out and gazes at his leathery fists.

The garden's magic is fading ... The eucalyptuses die of old age, the divine weeping willows have withered ... only the stubbornly romantic cypresses preserve the garden's ancient purity. Large grilles jut out from the walls, swing open and look down on the path. Wild flowers flourish among lordly lilies.

The garden will soon disappear. The creations of other centuries must be obliterated ... It is sad ... but the *fête galante* has ended. Death's icy carriages have taken those gentlemen and their ancient ladies away to another realm ... the pond stagnated and the heirs to those phantom families fried and ate the swans when they were hungry. Today's swans are not the same ... The silver boat furrowing the ethereal lake sank with its innocent contingent of shy lovers. The shepherds were transformed into wild beasts. Marchioness Eulalia stopped laughing. It is relentless! First the nymphs vanished. Then the marchionesses and abbots, now perhaps the poets will die ...

The columns crumbled as the arbours and statues next to the roses crumble now ... The story of the ravaged maiden, who entered the order of Saint Clare, was lost forever ...

Pretty little ragamuffins play down one of the avenues among the gardening implements ... They're ripping up a large tome that has coloured prints of eighteenth-century ladies and gentlemen ... a parody of Victor Hugo's martyrdom of Saint Bartholomew ... behind them an exhausted, half-starved mother sits on the ground and mends clothes.

Silence filled the garden ...

Two young men came in through the main gate. One began to shout enthusiastically. It was all so beautiful! He would sit there and dream a while ... but his young companion, waving a repulsive book of statistics, exclaimed in horror: 'Don't be so silly! Can't you see this place is most unhygienic! Let's be off,' and off they went ... There's no cure, the party passed this way but is never going to return ... The madrigal died with the birth of the railway. Sighs of love inspired by a passionate stanza, gallant mottoes on buttons, lute serenades, departed with their century ... Silks, lace, vases and cameo broaches have sunk without trace. All that survives is the garden ... the graveyard for all that ... protected by cypresses ... with fountains that preserve the water from the same era, statues that fade from view because they would rather not see us ... houses with boarded up balconies ...

Another romantic stepped through the window and was struck dumb with admiration. He half-closed his eyes as if the garden were a daydream ... but left immediately. He had an office to go to ... The children on the avenue continued their work of destruction ... and their mother sang pleasantly enough ... 'Does this garden belong to you?' and they answer, 'No sir, it's the Marchioness's ... but she's so kind she's given it to us so we can plant out an allotment.' 'How appalling! What a pity about this garden!' I exclaim. 'I can see,' says the mother, 'you are well fed! If only you knew how little we earn! At least if we change this garden into an allotment, we can sell lettuces and cabbages in the city and my children will have a bit more to eat ...' Her skeletal offspring continue their labours ... The mother sighs, 'How I wish we didn't have to eat so!' 'You know what I think,' I answer, 'it's time this garden was gone.'

It is inevitable, the festivities are over ... Verlaine weeps and Édouard Dubus plays his black violin ... The plough will soon enter the garden's wonderfully shady bowers ... It is inevitable.

A Garden That Has Died

It is a rainy morning in the garden ... The worm-eaten door into the abandoned precinct stands at the foot of a muddy slope next to a cross that damp has turned green and black. Beyond that a grey stone bridge and in the misty distance a snowy mountain. A river flows gently between crags, humming its ancient song along the valley floor.

Two old men in torn capes are warming themselves over a struggling charcoal fire in a hovel next to the door ... The inside of the precinct is desolate and harrowing. The rain intensifies this impression. It is easy to slip. The ground is littered with big dead tree-trunks ... The high, yellow walls are criss-crossed by huge cracks from which lizards trace enigmatic arabesques. At the back the remains of a cloister overgrown by ivy and withered flowers, its columns leaning. Yellow flowers covered in raindrops grow out of crannies in the crumbling stone; on the ground, puddles of damp in the grass ...

Of the fine cloisters that once beheld processions with gold monstrances between solemn, magnificent tapestries, only the high walls remain ...

A column has collapsed on the fountain, and when it celebrated its nuptials of stone, loving moss spread its delicate mantels over them. Small blades of bright green grass peer out of the holes in the capital lying on the ground.

Plants intertwine and ivy covers the old columns that still stand; water spills over the side of the fountain, licks the surrounding stone floor and surrenders to the earth that drinks it in disgust ... The rest disappears down a black hole that drinks eagerly.

Thick curtains of cobwebs and ferns drape the stone benches ... You can hear a relentless drip-drip ... water lamenting the sadness in our dead garden. There is nothing new there ... even the water's always the same... it seeps into the ground and re-surfaces out of the statue in the fountain.

Walking is impossible because climbing plants tangle with your feet ... as if the garden's hidden genii wanted to grasp something living among so much desolation and death ... A pantheon lies behind the remains of the cloister. The tombs have disappeared ... faded lettering between cobwebs and shadows merely reveals a Latin inscription ... only two words are visible, *Requiescit* and the other *Mortuos* ...

The rain turns heavier and falls on the garden in a dull, muffled sound ... Some large leaves shake gently and a large lizard pokes out its flattened head, runs and hides under some stones. Its tail sticks out but it soon pulls it in ... The grass flattened by the lizard's weight lazily straightens itself. The breeze rustles the yellow flowers, shakes the water off their petals ... Snails cling to the walls ... Time has been merciless towards this garden: it has withered its rose-bushes and privet and breathed life into treacherous, evil-smelling plants ...

The rain keeps falling.

Station Gardens

These are peculiar and poverty-stricken. They have acacia trees and are surrounded by black fences ... These gardens would prefer to be quiet and restful ... so many anxious, edgy eyes have peered at them! Gardens have always been restful, melancholy places. The eternal silence of gardens sung by poets ... but a station garden is the height of stress. They speed quickly past our eyes and we don't even see them ... When we travel, we focus our imaginations on distant places, and they can't catch our attention. The plants have withered. Boxwood encroaches on flowerbeds from which bell-flower creepers scale the wall ... The green of the garden has a distinct black tinge ... Smoke has left its sooty traces on the foliage. Some have rickety vines supported by wire.

On one side is the canteen. All alcoholic leftovers are poured on the garden: these flowers are watered with stinking wine.

Trains pass quickly through and a garden that longs for solitude and pleasant sounds hears the loud whistle-blasts of trains, the solemn hiss of steam and the squeak of chains and wheels. These shapely flowers and acacias are not where they would like to be.

The garden sees so many dreamy, half-shut eyes rush by and stare vacantly out. The plants sway gently to the strong gusts of wind from the trains.

At night feeble yellow street lamps provide a deathly light.

In one of these humble, sooty little gardens a tea rose grows. Such a plant in the desolation all around is almost a miracle ... but the frail roses open their wondrous topaz only to be given a black disguise by coal dust and soot.

None the less, it was clear that it *was* a tea rose ... But one day when I walked through the station, the rose-bush was transformed. A hideous black stained the delicate, scented flowers ... the canteen woman had tipped her coffee grouts over the bush ... An astonished girl asks me, 'What flowers are those?' and I reply sadly, 'Roses! my child, roses ...!' Then the train moved off.

VARIATIONS ON A THEME

❖ ❖ ❖ ❖ ❖

Often when we walk through these places associated with remote legends we perceive solitary tracts of land where our soul would like to rest eternally ... Their magical spell stems from the fact that we stroll by their expanse unaware of the mysteries they hide. Some emotional states are so strange! When we find ourselves in a pleasant spot we would prefer to spend our lifetime there re-creating ourselves in its beauty... But then we depart, not really sure why ... When we travel we see an endless series of frescoes by nature, people, colours and sounds our minds would like to grasp and etch on our souls, but we are petty and forget quite unconsciously. Before even contemplating a wonder we have heard about, we fantasise the form it might adopt in our dreams, and dream so hard it becomes impossible ... and that is why we are almost disappointed when we finally do see a renowned monument. We travel through cities and countryside, hardly ever stop, eyes always open, trying to retain and feel everything, but soon become drowsy, exhausted and bored.

After taking a rest, those impressions begin to re-appear, one in all its splendour, another vague and blurred, yet another where our memories have the dying fall of twilight, in a bluish haze misting over everything we saw ... One set of impressions soon erases another and wreaks havoc amid the images that stand out ... a woman's face, a sunlit tower, the sea ...

Ruins

For Fernando Vílchez, such a generous, affable artist

The astonished traveller halts in front of the ruins.

He gazes at the ancient spectacle of a ruined fortress and feels numb and weary. The essence from a thousand sad colours spreads across royal mantles of ivy, over broken arches, through doorways into spaces overgrown by nettles and scattered with fallen capitals and onto high abandoned walls.

The scenario of a ruin is magnificent ... Light enters through collapsed roofs and finds nowhere to reflect ... it can only penetrate the hovels in a gallery open to the countryside or a cloister, softening the tone of the shadows.

The contrast between the greens and the golds gently caressed by the light creates an astonishing spectrum from the mute to the embittered.

Echoes are another of the charms of ruins.

Echoes that disappear in open country nest in devastated

corners, in cellars full of wild creepers.

In ruins on plains echoes lurk in the most recondite crevices. On vast, empty plains these little genii have no place to rest and, when an ancient building collapses, they enter dead rooms and mock every sound, guffaw and scream in despair and slur their conversations in a vomit of words.

Ruins slowly sink into the ground until they are completely buried and the invisible characters that once lived there depart; echoes dance over the plains again, sleep in order to wake another day. The scenario is submerged and the legend ends. Birds fly to a more agreeable place, snakes flee to more out-of-the-way burrows and, when the ruin sinks completely, the historical tragedy is over ...

Ruins wear the badge of fear rather than badges of art, adornment and romance.

The friars or lords who inhabited these castles fled, but one night a peasant straggler returning late to the hamlet sees a great white figure in the wild undergrowth and two greenish, languid eyes, then hears cries from those being eternally tortured in the castle dungeons and chains being dragged along empty passageways ... The peasant runs off, recounts what he has seen and the entire village is panic-stricken ... The ruins are haunted! Now no one visits them and they gleam in the dark ... One stormy night, an old village woman shoos away the children and by the fireside relates to the neighbours a story from the past her great-great-grandmother once told her. A story of love and fairies from the time when the ruin was inhabited ... The white ghost who appeared must be the lady who became a nun after she killed her husband ... they all cross themselves ... On another night, another neighbour says the ghost was rowing down the river in the pale moonlight ... Then a storm broke ...

All ruins have frightening stories. Some are connected; others have already been forgotten.

Ruins evoke frightening ballads of wandering spirits.

The whole of Romantic literature locates its figures of fantasy in ruins ... because they give ruins their spirit: a very big, nay a huge white ghost that weeps at night, while under the ivy stones crumble to the gentle lapping of water.

Fresdelval

The landscape is quiet and restful. Hills and holm-oaks. Red and grey spaces. Green roads snaking up distant hills and vast solitude.

The demolished monastery reclines on a sloping hillside fenced in by green-black elms. All around, gentle inclines of faded weeds and promontories that are almost hills, from where one can survey the magnificent, bronzed spectacle.

The nearest hills are harsh and red; in the distance poplar groves blotch the opaque mists ... the blind windows of an ancient convent peer out from peaceful elms. It has the magnificent allure of a religious legend. It was born from an aristocratic line of kings and princes. The protagonist is a captive Moor converted to Christianity ... but these places have lost their legendary aura. The most graceful arches still stand and shore up green clumps of ivy. There are decapitated medallions. Gothic rose windows gently filter the light. Wild flowers and weeds have taken over the ruin ... A large green-grey patch of damp extends along the Gothic cloister ... A strictly Castilian corner could act as backcloth to a pale-eyed character wearing a cape ... all that remains of a Renaissance cloister that is the height of simplicity. Sturdy columns, squat arches and a large eave. The background is black and the floor a host of weeds, in front there is an abandoned cart and rotting wooden mangers, beyond that an unhinged door, a cowbell, ivy and weeping willows ... Nearby a severed column looks at its reflection in a pond ... All is quiet in the afternoon. This landscape is deeply chaste.

A Village

A walk through a Castilian village in the silence of the afternoon, the sun gilds the languid church tower and humble houses. Old people sit next to the entrance. They are like stone figures in an intensely religious ceremony. One occasionally moves a hand. Doors shut ... Beehives stick out of the flowers ... An ugly woman feeds a piglet. Long poles lean forlornly over stockyard walls. They are lances in waiting. On the way out of the village bulls drink from an almost stagnant pond ... Red twilight mists begin to rise in the distance.

A Passing City

Blue sky. Sunny tranquillity. Gleaming white sheep scramble between the gums of fortified walls and leave a vaporous haze of silver in their wake. The city rings its metallic horns as mellifluous as immeasurable honey.

Wrought iron ... Explosions of solemnity. Austere, noble, rather squat, their bells still, the lordly churches profiled against the smoke curling from chimneys are triumphs of Romanticism, their weathervanes are crosses, hearts or snakes, their realm of gold hidden under mossy green ... The hills' monstrous claws are like yellow opals ... The light shimmers over the medieval city ... Things are in musical repose ... It is a bright morning.

A Renaissance Palace

A spacious, deserted square ... spindly, old trees. A white façade has a chipped, worm-eaten font the pipes of which haven't seen water in a long time ... The ground is overgrown by weeds and grass. There is an empty niche in one corner ... The palace is at the back of the square.

Finding such aristocratic magnificence next to poor hovels in this moribund spot creates a strange impression ... The palace is beautifully golden ... It has large, noble balconies, serpents coil round its columns, frightened medusas and fantastic tritons.

Lunatic cortèges travel the friezes full of wit and movement that disappear into the stone as time goes by.

The processions include naked men holding bouquets of roses over their sexes and women pouting lasciviously, their arms writhing snakes that transform into acanthus leaves, and a cascade of bobbles. Sea monsters with tree-like horns and hands of flowers stop them in their tracks, open their mouths and chase everyone away. Some flee ridiculously and others rest their hands gravely on their chests. This decorative forest of flowers and figures is protected by a beautifully carved eave, sustained by huge supports populated by unkempt giants, mastiffs, noble faces, among foliage of smaller faces, daisies, diamonds and tiny goat heads ... A heart-shaped weathervane crowns the palace; by its side, a tall cypress tree.

Procession

And above the altar of the holy martyrs, where those who became blood and flames because of love for Jesus are at rest, and above the silver ark that the mystical glass gave a celestial hue, the priest in white and purple raiments uncovered the ancient chalice, knelt and took communion ... The organ wept melancholy tears to Gounod. Incense spluttered affectionately and bells pealed languidly above the hollow sound of dragging feet ... The canopy, that pinnacle of gravitas, and the golden, emerald-encrusted cross swayed slowly to the tragic lilt of Latin verse, while the organ recited its poem of suffering and swooning ... The procession sighed and descended from the sacred altar into the light and the priests' pallid hands gripped sturdy candles and walked in step to a melody from a distant century ... Deep bass sub-chanters proclaimed sententiously, a sextet of choirboys dispatched high notes to semi-circular arches, vergers beat their staffs on the ground and sweet censers clashed chains as they swung through the air ... And all in a haze of grey mist from the incense dispersed by a cold draught ... The procession moved through massive wrought-bronze grilles, its candles tinged in topaz, opened a door carved by ingenuous hands and entered a cloister suffused with muted colours ... On the walls, black-eyed Byzantine statues, dusty parchment bearing a papal bull or prayer from the past, icy tombs of knights bearing marble weapons and rigid ladies with lions at their feet ... The cortège entered the cloister to a melodious dirge from the bassoon and a sleepy Gregorian chant ...

When the monks walk by a tomb, they halt and solemnly declaim responses that echo around the vaults like screams of terror ... Now they stop and pray before a recumbent bishop. They all recite a funeral dirge and then fall silent ... At that very moment, the ministrant bringing up the rear sings a dreadful verse in a distant voice ... The incense throws up a milky blur of light and the procession resumes in quiet prayer and the cathedral's maddening soul cries out to the sound of dragging feet ... The solitary altar, lined by tall candles and *repoussé* silver trimming, waits for the ministrant to reveal its spiritual allure ... A Virgin seated on a throne listens out for the minister of the Lord to start his prayer and the host remains in suspense until invoked ... White-wigged mace-bearers in damask tunics walk towards the altar, rows of priests in the richest fabrics process, and finally the bishop makes an appearance, the bearer of the relics ... When they reach the altar, the music stops, the individual in purple mumbles words that are unintelligible. Bells chime, people kneel and he lifts a glass and copper urn containing a blackened, dried-out tibia up into the heavy silks of incense. The city clock strikes twelve and the monsters in the choir smile their eternal smile, as always.

Castilian Dawn

The night fog has yet to lift. A shaft of white light opens on the horizon and floods the expanse of ploughed earth with bright shadows. The cold poplars look at themselves in the blue-green mirrors of the irrigation channels.

Peace and harmony reign. Distant mountains string out in soft black shapes, the land hides in low clouds of fog and dewy drizzle falls from wan skies ...

The abyss of twilight turns a ruddy pink ... A village raises its tower, which looks down towards a distant rose. The wind begins its dance over the plain ... A far-off train whistles and an abandoned ploughshare sticks up above a tract of fallow land ...

Convent

The convent is outside the city. Its portico is fronted by a sorry stretch of terrain. Like all convent land, it is full of hollyhocks, a white jasmine that is scentless in order to be sinless, and aristocratic ivies. A place for meditation and nunnish melancholy. A strident, solemn bell rings out to announce that there is a visitor.

You enter a visiting room as modest as a village girl's bedroom, with its baked clay saints, blackened prints of Virgins vaguely moustached by runny old inks, and lots of woodworm. Highly curious nuns scrutinise the traveller, question him, advise him and, laughing and tittering, show him all the relics they possess.

They give him cakes filled with angel's hair jam and describe a scene from their lives inside. On Saturday nights they gather round the light from the only oil-lamp and, seated on cork matting, weave their habits on age-old distaffs. One narrates and the rest listen in saintly silence ... Meanwhile, fear and legends resonate across cloisters and courtyards, and urge the wind to play its bassoon in the bass key of F.

Fields

It is mid-afternoon and the sun shines in passionate bursts. A July afternoon, a fortress tower and ripe corn ... The breeze rustles softly through reddish yellow fields ... A scythe occasionally glints ... Poppies around the edges and elms and sheep on the hills. Some fields are sown with silvery oats. A waxing moon walks almost invisibly across the sky ... The figure of an old shepherd is profiled against a hillside and the sun gives the religious ambience a transparent gold hue and fills the distant blue with a mystical aura ... Their gentle eyes half-closed, oxen progress majestically in front of a cart's languid to-and-fro. Smells of corn and sun impregnate the air. The wonder of the afternoon is in the iridescent backcloth. From time to time you glimpse a far-off stone tower where swallows swoop and cheep-cheep, and colourless villages that surge out of the hills, as if by magic.

Noon in August

The only sound in the vast field is the dying cicada, inebriated by the light and its own song.

It is noon. The air shimmers in the heat. You catch a glimpse of green-black poplar groves behind the sheet of fire over the fields. The countryside is deserted. The labourers are asleep in their houses. The water-runs whisper mysteriously to one another. Blown by the wind, ears of corn rub against each other and make a silvery sound. A poppy field is withering through lack of water. The great symphony of light makes it impossible to open your eyes.

The curfew bell tolls in the country's peaceful silence, voluptuous chimes ... Issuing a challenge to the flesh ...

Village women bathe in the river. They cry out in pleasure

when they feel the cool water licking their bellies and breasts. Young lads lurk like fauns in the undergrowth and watch them naked. Nature would prefer a giant copulation. Bees buzz monotonously. The lads writhe between the flowers and weeping willow when they see a lass emerge naked from the water, breasts pert, twisting her hair while the other girls tease her, splashing her belly …

A quail sings in the cornfield.

Work begins on the threshing floors. A breeze blows. Winnowing-forks pitch the straw high into the sky. The golden grain falls to the ground and the breeze blows away the straw which falls, covering everything. Mules run over the threshing floor. The hazy landscape oppresses and the distant hills drown in a shimmering sea of white haze. Some naked brown children bathe in a water-run, come out and wallow in the hot dust on the road. Carts arrive, heaving under their load of corn … There is a smell of dry wheat.

A Romantic Visit: Santa María de las Huelgas

An ivory charm opened and revealed a mirage of emotions, like a tale from the Orient … The nuns wore white habits and black veils, and their small pink and placid faces peered from beneath the most elegant turbans. Behind them a tortured Christ in a gallery … The whole of the medieval aristocracy is enclosed in these ancient, noble cloisters … Which smell as if they've been wiped down by a white cloth and are still slightly damp.

cloisteRs, Sta Maria de las Huelgas

On that July afternoon, the forlorn, weed-covered courtyard, its windows half-closed, rustles peacefully in the sun. They bury the nuns under the cloister's charming, bluish Gothic tiles ... The chapter-house, which reminds you of Poblet, houses the portraits of abbesses long gone, slender, aristocratic figures, their remarkably white, distinguished hands gripping staffs that are like huge silvery flowers ... Nuns rush along the far ends of the cloister, trailing their skirts behind them. Oriental tiles gleam and glint in the galleries.

The visit began and, invoked by nunnish music, a murky era of Spanish history appeared, an era of legends and unknown but magical deeds the faith and devoted love of those women have preserved, Alfonso VIII and San Fernando, Doña Berenguela and Sancho the Desired ... and princesses, children and knights, all placed in simple tombs touching the walls, and tales of princess-nuns who died in saintly odour ... and the Battle of Las Navas and the cross carried by Archbishop Don Rodrigo ... and we reached the choir, where you find the heart of the community ...

It is spacious and imposing ... a frightening Calvary lurks at the back, imbuing the silence with pity ... Luminous windows in distant vaults soften the shock ... Pink and light blue tapestries cover the walls, recounting the deeds of Roman emperors ...

Everything the nuns say of the dead they say with genuine unctuous gratitude. Alfonso, from the battle of Las Navas, is apparently a saint in their eyes ... and they point sadly to Alfonso the Wise's empty tomb and naïvely express astonishment in front of the tomb of the Infanta Berenguela, who on a fatal day for the convent was found sitting on a stairway in the choir ... The melancholy-faced abbess recites affectionately and instructively the miracles wrought by the medieval Infanta's mummy ... We walk through the tawny gold Romanesque courtyard, its fountain full of sunbeam arabesques and simple flowers ... and back to the main choir, where we saw delightful, almost nunnishly innocent Virgins ...

Then a nun released the train of her habit, peacock-like,

Gothic tomb, Sta Maria de las Huelgas

confessional, sᵗᵃ María de Las Huelgas

as huge as the *Pomme d'anis* by Francis Jammes, and I left the convent when the bells rang for prayer ... Dairy cows, their bells tinkling, ambled past. The water in the irrigation channels was still and a refreshing breeze blew from the cornfields ... My heart suddenly felt drowsy after such a devout afternoon.

Another Convent

Whenever I approach a convent, I do so with religious hope and sadness ... They strike the loudest note of oblivion in these forgotten cities. I am sure forgetfulness is the great problem stirring in these enormous edifices ...

We continually hope to find something spiritual or full of beauty so we can unburden our souls of their main source of sorrow ... and we always hasten, impelled by desire for that impossible happiness ... We almost never achieve such a state: form alone varies; essences remain unchanged.

Childishly frail, the nuns shut themselves in the convent and wall up the path to oblivion ... They transform what they are trying to forget into what is most present in their souls.

A huge failure of feeling throbs throughout the church ... The heart rules all.

Crystalline fountains often spurt from distant lips in the nuns' chaste imaginations ... When I enter the church, the nuns, who are praying quietly, scatter through the choir liked scared pigeons to gaze at me. How sad! Their wimples are like white stumps and the squat choir looks as if it would rather sink … A nun coughs … There are large paintings of forgotten people on the wall, beautiful, dark-skinned Virgins with a touch of Rubens, against warm backgrounds of orangey clouds … Lurid, nunnish flowers stand on the altars, a sensual, religious scent of dogwood floats in the air … We walk down passages with a *via crucis* and gleaming urns to the visiting room … The nuns are like faces without a body that speak chastely in voices that diffuse an intense diluted smell …

The grille to the visiting room has sharp iron prongs that threatened to pierce us in the eye … The nuns speak their names one by one … Mother Love … Mother Heart …

There is a pot of red carnations on a sideboard … in front of a caged canary.

Dusk

The light opens everything up to the wonderful colour of the moment … The countryside that earlier had resisted the unrivalled might of a June afternoon now bathes in delicate shades and displays a quiet melody of colour. The foothills of the mountains turn blue, while the rocky peaks are still a whitish hue … The light keeps modulating the shades like a precious stone, until it is a fantastic pink fire that gradually changes into a yellow dust with soft topaz tints. The only green is in the poplar groves and on the lip of the irrigation channel … The severe, handsome sun, silhouetted against the blue of the sky, sinks vaguely into the firm navel of a mountain's monstrous belly.

The August air shivers ... a sweet light invades everywhere ... Reapers walk along the steep slopes singing cheerfully ... The old, battered chapel bells ring the Angelus ... The stars begin to shine. A train's steely crescendo rushes through the groves of holm-oak ... Dogs bark and cartwheels collide and clash in the distance ... Nightfall.

Sunday Evening in a Large Village

First deep, restful silence and ineffable peace ... broken only by birds screeching from the acacias or a cart squeaking down the deserted street ... Then, when the sun tried to set, doors started to open and pleasantly powdered girls peered out, flowers in their hair ...

Boys came out onto a narrow street, keeping their arms still for fear they might spoil their brand new suits; girls walked arm in arm down the middle of the street gripping their handkerchiefs. The village stroll was a lively affair. The dust thrown up by the passers-by floated on the air under the tall poplars ... Flushed, dark-skinned girls strutted shamelessly, proud of their bright silk blouses, fake gold chains and huge, trembling breasts. The boys' glances eagerly followed them, half-closing their eyes and hiding their faces behind their hats.

They were loud, attractive girls, with fresh, sensual lips and magnificent black tresses ... The water spouting from the fountain made the still, gentle water in the trough sizzle.

Twilight began to glow divinely in the sky. The clouds were the gentle hue of translucent roses ... On a street-corner, between white roses and clumps of morning glory, a betrothed couple chatted, brought their heads together eager for a kiss ... Some envious lasses watched them out of the corner of an eye ... That heavenly languid evening merited a passionate lovers' kiss! On a grey stone seat that glints like a mirror, a scabby, parchment-skinned old woman was amusing a fair-skinned baby who was anxiously waving a hand, wanting to cut a rose that bobbed serenely among the branches ... A group of girls behind them hugged one another's waists and sang an old ballad of love and war, out of tune ... A great buzz of conversation floated on the breeze ... The band struck up in a rickety old wooden bandstand ... Its musicians were a curious, entertaining bunch: one wasn't in uniform; the rest wore them ragged ... A *habanera* from a Spanish operetta vibrated through the air ... trite and melancholy, sentimental and loathsome ... Many melodies that visit our soul hurt our emotions with such contrasts ... The tuba and key-bugles sustained the languid, almost oriental rhythm ... Sometimes, the musicians made technical mistakes or blew incorrectly ... The clarinet launched into horrific guffaws, vamping the tune outlandishly ... The poor musicians were really working hard! One or two were exhausted and dripped sweat ... Only the drummer, a stern, serious fellow, occasionally tapped his instrument ... and looked at their audience as if delighted by what he was doing ... The leader of the band, an oldish man with a stiff moustache and prominent paunch, conducted with lots of panache, waving his hands to the beat of the *habanera*, gesturing imperiously to the man on the kettle-drum to make a dramatic entry, arching his bushy eyebrows, rolling his eyes when he switched the melody to a minor key before repeating the theme ... The flute-player was near the maestro, a short overweight fellow with bright, beady eyes ... who blew with great élan, his eyes bulging to bursting point ... He played a drawn-out solo, which caused the maestro to half-close his eyes in pure bliss and the audience to listen in awe ... A smelly old man in rags next to me exclaimed, 'He's the best of the bunch ... he were born that way, he's got it in his blood, don't y' think?' ... I stared at the wretched musician, and it was a source of great joy to watch that ball of flesh with mousey eyes swaying with pleasure and it seemed extraordinary that he should be holding a flute. That gallant, noble instrument, that aristocratic, literary tube, brother to the lyre and panpipe, its prestige confirmed by the century of lace and harpsichords ... was in hairy Stone Age clutches that roughed up the notes ... The *habanera* was interminable ... The girls sang words where the sun, lilies, palm-trees and blondes paraded by ... The boys whistled along loudly ...

A young blood out of synch with that scene sat on a chair, his hands in his pockets, gazing at the crowd, smugly superior ... Some girls laughed at his sleek hair and the belt squeezing his waist ... It was getting late, the band stopped playing and the street emptied out ... The church bell began ringing for Rosary ... The band struck up again, and people began to make their way home ... The twilight sun coloured the weathervanes red. Everything else was already in darkness … The workers started to arrive in the village, tired and ragged, walking slowly, hoes over shoulders, heads bowed … Behind came gentle, rested flocks, raising a cloud of dust in their wake and tinkling their bells … then a drove of frisky mules that made the frightened little girls run off, and soft, woolly colts neighed in anticipation of their stable's warm comforts … The whole air was filled with the noise of bells, braying, bleating and neighing … And finally the pigs entered the village, grunting fiercely and running to their respective homes, chased by mistresses who scattered a trail of a maize or beans to lure them back to their sties … The village fell silent once more … The priest walked down the empty road on his way to evening prayers. A young kid came whistling by, holding a can of oil.

Two devout old women going to Rosary prayers drew contorted black squiggles against glaringly white walls … before they plunged into the mouth of the church door … Dinner was being cooked on village hearths. Two large, light brown and placid cows dragged their udders along the road that led to the fields … Two boys hurried them along with their sticks … A guitar twanged and in a rich man's house an old piano played Czerny monotonously.

An Abandoned Church

The church rising above the outskirts of the dead city has for some time been bereft of incense and an organ's sweet caress … It is a ruin where it is impossible to worship …

Solemn ceremonies when the canopy swayed in sweet-smelling mists and rich chasubles glinted in the darkness have forsaken the church. Today its only inhabitants are a number of wretched saints down on their luck, abandoned there as useless ... All that remains on the main altarpiece is a sculpture of Saint Mark holding a bull without horns ... The church is cold and frightening, with dirty, flaking saints who snarl sardonically ... These temples are appalling, full of blank, miserable expressions, figures reclining on walls, rotten flesh beaten black and blue, mouths drooping from a sense of inferiority ...

The only thing of beauty is a forgotten medallion in which a Hellenic Virgin gives a blessing with a fractured hand while pointing at the Child, who in turn looks lovingly at her.

The medallion is beautiful ... Its alabaster is flecked with faded gold ... Tall weeds, fig trees, wild hollyhocks and ancient pitimini roses besiege the building ... The church guardians stand in the doorway, a couple of filthy, bleary-eyed women with a mysterious, sibylline air.

Pause

Under the romantic tree *par excellence*, the precious flower of our heart opens out to the infinite tranquillity that follows death ... Silence can never give us the keys to that immense path ... The waning chords of a dying orchestra will perhaps help our heart learn to suffer its unknown calvary with elegance.

Silence has its own music, but sound holds the essence of the music of silence … The heart has to resolve the terrible dilemma … Faced by a splendid vision of empty, sonorous fields, the soul foretells something of its solitude. Women with unkempt hair walk along the red road of the imagination. They smile at us, are ours in their mouths; we pour out our souls and smile with a disturbing, dream-like tranquillity.

They will be ours, but we will be stones and flowers and our thought … Oh, our thought …! Our entire soul wants to spread across the fields and settle on distant pine groves to the black velvet lilt of their music … A flock with exhausted bells passes by in the distance, accompanied by an old man with sunken eyes. There are clouds in the sky that are like huge blocks of unfamiliar marble … and our imagination runs riot, opens a path of pleasurable sorrows …

The moon appears majestically between the hills. Welcome, companion to the sensual, smitten traveller. Greetings, old friend and consoler of the sad. Handmaiden of poets. Refuge for the passionate. Perverse, chaste rose. Ark of sensuality and mysticism. Infinite artist in a minor key. Greetings, tranquil beacon of love and lamentation! Oh fields! How you are reborn into another world under the moon …

Silence is but grieving thought and death … That horrendous path opens before us and we have perforce to walk there …

A Hospice in Galicia

It is autumn in Galicia and the rain is falling silently and slowly on the gentle green land. Sometimes pine-covered hills emerge from hazy, slumbering clouds. The city is quiet. The poor, humble hospice faces a green-black stone church where the hedge-mustard would like its flowers to flourish ... The damp front door gives an impression of neglect ... Inside, it smells of poorly seasoned food and extreme poverty. The courtyard is Romanesque ... The inmates, rachitic, emaciated children with bleary eyes and stiff hair, are playing in the middle. Many are quite fair, but illness gives their heads strange colorations ... Pale, with sunken chests, pallid lips, bony hands, they walk or play with one another under Galicia's eternal drizzle ... Some, who are sicklier, don't join in and sit still in recesses, eyes motionless in their little, infirm heads. Another is lame and insists on jumping over little rocks on the ground ... Nuns come and go, rushing to the sound of their rosary beads. There is a musty rose in one corner.

All their faces are painfully sad; one might say they have presentiments of approaching death ... This huge, squat entrance door has seen endless processions of human spectres enter anxiously and abandon their children ... I feel sorry for this door through which so many of the wretched have passed ... It must know what its mission is and want to die of grief, because it is worm-eaten, filthy and unhinged ... One day perhaps it will take pity on hungry children and serious social injustice and collapse dramatically on a municipal charity commission, crushing on the spot so many frock-coated bandits in order to make one of those beautiful omelettes Spain so sorely needs ... A hospice that seems uninhabited, except for these rachitic, pain-wracked children. The heart feels a great need to weep and a tremendous desire for equality ...

An elegantly dressed gentleman walks along a whitewashed gallery, followed by nuns, looking impassively to his right and left. The children doff their caps respectfully, full of fear. He is the representative of charity ... A bell rings... The door opens noisily, courageously ... When it shuts, it swings slowly to, as if it were crying ... The rain never stops ...

A Romance by Mendelssohn

The port is quiet. Boats bob sleepily on the blue honeyed sea. In the distance a city's towers and the rocky slopes of the mountains ... It is the twilight hour and lights come on in boats and houses ... You see clusters of buildings inverted in the shimmering, golden zigzags of the reflections on the waves ... There is a pleasant, soft, lunar colour on the water ... The quayside is soon silent and deserted ... Two burly men in blue walk by, arguing heatedly ... The *romanza* without words drifted over the air from a distant piano ... A marvellous *romanza* full of the romantic spirit of 1830 ... It began slowly with delicious *rubato*, then unleashed a song bursting with passion. The melody sometimes went silent as the bass notes wove soft, austere harmonies ... The music reached the port, enfolding everything in a fascinating emotional sound. The close-packed waves fell voluptuously as they licked the steps of the pier ... The piano was still playing the *romanza* when night fell. A ghostly white boat drifted over leaden green waters to the slow rhythm of the oars.

Streets in an Ancient City

Dirty streets with withered weeds, crumbling houses, stolen gargoyles, headless saints, no more than a pile of stones. Entrances with *repoussé* columns, pockmarked medallions, Roman wreaths ... On one dark street, a water trough submerged under pale coloured flowers.

Another street has low porticos, sad women, damp iron grilles and sagging arches ... Many balconies are collapsing under the weight of daisies and geraniums that are blinding lights in the powerful summer sun ... Seashells on façades ... Small, windowless palaces with moon-shaped doorknockers.

White houses without a pane of glass in their balconies. Magnificent churches with austere, gilded stone candlesticks, altars wreathed in skulls, sumptuous, exuberant entrances where brawny men fight winged bulls, scowling youths peer through baskets of curious leaves, and men and animals emerge from the acanthus decorating gilded capitals. Façades overflow with motifs from which children spring with serpents' tongues locking deformed hands, the muscular arms of lascivious, busty matrons supporting columns full of Latin mottoes and memorable dates, oriental dancers in provocative poses, cold, mocking helmet crests, chubby angels flying over griffins and caryatids, sad faces with closed eyes ...

When walking through deserted, melancholy squares ... sounds of school drift by ... In one, children chant, 'The holy fathers who were awaiting the Holy Advent ...'

At the end of the streets fields shimmer under the blistering summer sun.

The Duero

The river flows green and gentle through Zamora. The huge bald Byzantine dome gazes at itself in the deep waters ... Boats float slowly by on the waves.

In the distance, drab hills peer out from the grey-brown terrain ... Small Romanesque churches descend the narrow streets to the river ... that slowly hauls along its prestigious burden of historic scenes to the gentle *bass continuo* of the waves ...

The ancient romantic story of the river is at an end ... Nothing remains of what the river once saw ... The story has fallen silent ... But the old Duero dreams solemnly on and still sees blurry heroes battling in a ballad.

ENVOI

✤ ✤ ✤ ✤ ✤

For my dear teacher Don Martín Domínguez Berrueta and my dear companions, Paquito López Rodríguez, Luis Mariscal, Ricardo Gómez Ortega, Miguel Martínez Carlón and Rafael Martínez Ibáñez who accompanied me on my travels.

GLOSSARY

✤ ✤ ✤ ✤ ✤

Gaspar Becerra (1520–1568): Artist and sculptor from Baeza who prospered in Rome in the 1540s and '50s before returning to Spain in 1562 as court painter to Philip II.

Mariano Benlliure (1862–1947): Valencian who worked on numerous religious sculptures and public monuments, enhancing the heroic virtues of Restoration politicians and members of the royal family such as Sagasta, María Cristina de Borbón and Alfonso XII.

Gonzalo de Berceo (c.1197–ante 1264): Born in Berceo near the Benedictine monastery of San Millán de la Cogolla in the Rioja; his verse praises to the Virgin Mary are traditionally seen as the first poems in Spanish by a named writer.

El Borgoñón: Felipe Bigarny (c.1475–1542), born in Burgundy, made his reputation as a sculptor in Spain; he was in charge of the sculptures for Burgos Cathedral, where he carved, amongst other works, the tomb of Canon Gonzalo Díaz de Lerma.

Julio Burell (1859–1919): Journalist and conservative politician who was MP for La Coruña and Jaén and Minister for Education and the Fine Arts during the reign of Alfonso XII.

Saints Cosmas and **Damian**: Third-century Christian physicians from Cilicia, in present-day Turkey, who brought many to the faith by their free treatment of patients. They were tortured and executed for refusing to renege on their beliefs.

Édouard Dubus (1864–1895): Minor French Symbolist poet, admired by the Nicaraguan writer Rubén Darío. He died of an overdose of morphine after writing 'When Violins Die' and numerous poems to faded roses and melancholy.

El Españoleto: José de Ribera (1591–1652) lived and painted mainly in Naples, where he was nicknamed 'Lo Spagnoletto'. He was influenced by Caravaggio and renowned for his religious figures and naturalistic depictions of daily life.

Domenico Fancelli (1469–1519): Italian who worked primarily in Spain. In 1510 he was commissioned to sculpt the tomb of Prince Don Juan, the prematurely deceased heir to Isabel and Ferdinand, for the Royal Monastery of Saint Thomas in Ávila, and in 1517 completed the tomb of the monarchs themselves in the Royal Chapel in Granada Cathedral.

Count Fernán González (c.910–970): Appears in 931 as Count of Burgos and Castile at the court of Ramiro II of León. He is celebrated as a patriotic hero for his role in the defeat of Abdelrahman III at the Battle of Simanacas in 939, and his deeds as 'the good Count' are praised in a thirteenth-century epic poem. He later fell out with Ramiro, was imprisoned and, some historians allege, fought alongside the Caliph of Córdoba. He built the tower in Covarrubias when it was briefly the capital of Castile in the tenth century.

Luis de Góngora y Argote (1561–1627): Baroque poet from Córdoba, author of *The Solitudes* and *The Fable of Poliphemus and Galatea*, and arch-enemy of Quevedo, who carped at his big nose and homosexuality. His writing was greatly admired by Lorca, who helped to rescue him from almost three centuries of oblivion.

Hatto, Bishop of Andernach (c.850–913): A Saxon bishop renowned for his cruelty and treachery. Southey wrote a ballad recounting his burning of the starving poor and how he himself was then devoured by rats.

Victor Hugo (1802–1885): In Hugo's *Quatrevingt-treize* (1874), a novel about the counter-revolution in Britanny in 1799 written shortly after the repression of the Paris Commune, there is a chapter ironically entitled 'The Massacre of St Bartholomew' in which children joyfully tear apart an antique illuminated book about the life of Saint Bartholomew, shredding the engravings and ripping the leather binding.

Doña Jimena (c.1046–1116): The wife of El Cid, whom he left with their daughters, Elvira and Sol, in the care of the Superior of the monastery of San Pedro de Cardeña when he went into exile, at least according to the epic poem. The remains of the Cid and his wife were buried in the monastery, but later moved to Burgos Cathedral.

Juan Ramón Jiménez (1881–1958): Andalusian poet and Nobel Prize winner (1956) whose early poetry is full of melancholy gardens, crumbling statues and withering flowers.

Juan de Juni (1506–1577): Born in France, trained there and in Italy, he became a major sculptor and architect in Spain, where he produced a number of stark, polychrome wood crucifixions.

Vicente Lampérez y Romea (1861–1923): Traditionalist architect, restorer and historian who wrote numerous tomes on Spanish monasteries and Christian architecture advocating a return to timeless Catholic values in style and design.

Le Comte de Lautréamont (1846–1870): Uruguayan-born French poet whose real name was Isidore Ducasse; author of *Les Chants de Maldoror* (1869) and other poetry in prose later championed by the Surrealists and the Situationists.

Juan Martínez Abades (1862–1920): Establishment

intellectual and artist, prolific painter of seascapes and composer of popular ditties such as 'In the Lift' and 'Water You Shouldn't Drink'.

Maurice Maeterlink (1862–1949): Belgian French writer of symbolist poetry and drama (*The Blue Bird*, 1908) and studies of natural life (*The Life of Ants*, 1939) whose fantasies fascinated Lorca.

El Montañés (1568–1649): Juan Martínez Montañés, Baroque sculptor and wood carver from Jaén sometimes called 'the king of wood'. His polychrome wood sculptures, including the hyperrealist Christ Crucified in Seville Cathedral, are to be seen in many southern churches,.

Naqsh-e Rustam: An important archaeological site near Persepolis in modern Iran, burial place of Darius the Great (ruled, 522–486 BC).

Manuel Pereira (1583–1683): Born in Oporto, he spent most his later life in Madrid and Castile. After a spell in a debtors' prison, he was recognised as a 'Familiar' of the Inquisition, a man of 'clean blood', and went on to create a large number of crucifixions and sculptures in wood like the Saint Bruno in the Cartuja de Miraflores.

Philip the Fair (1478–1506): Philip I of Spain. Born in Bruges, in 1496 he married the Infanta Joanna, daughter of Ferdinand and Isabel, in Liège. He aspired to the Spanish throne, but died of typhoid in 1506. Joanna the Mad was driven so by his infidelities and political ambitions; she gave birth to his six children.

Poblet: A Cistercian monastery west of Barcelona where the monks have followed the Rule of Saint Benedict since its foundation in 1150. The writer Josep Pla described its architectural jewels as representing 'a world of forms, traditions and symbols'.

Darío de Regoyos y Valdés (1857–1913): Painter from Asturias with a fondness for travelling throughout the Peninsula, who lived most of his life in Madrid. He developed from a style that favoured depictions of the dark side of Spanish history to one that verged on impressionism and pointillism.

Siloé: Gil de Siloé, el Maestre Gil, the leading sculptor in Burgos in the second half of the fifteenth century; his workshop was responsible for major works in the Cartuja de Miraflores. The alabaster tomb of Juan II and his wife Isabel of Portugal was commissioned by Queen Isabel as part of her drive to affirm her rule and took him four years to complete. His tomb of the Infante Don Alonso is renowned for its vegetable, animal and putti motifs.

The sublime Teresa: Saint Teresa of Ávila (1515–1582), a mystic and reformer of the Carmelite Order. Author of the first Spanish autobiography and many mystical works in prose and poetry fired by erotic imagery.

El Tostado: Bishop Alonso Fernández de Madrigal (1400–1455), known as 'el Tostado' because of his dark skin, was appointed Bishop of Ávila after successfully defending himself against charges of heresy. He wrote voluminously and 'to write more than el Tostado' became a proverbial expression for being long-winded. His marble tomb is in the apse of the cathedral.

Miguel de Unamuno (1864–1936): Basque poet, novelist and philosopher. His writings include a treatise of anguished Christian existentialism, *The Tragic Sense of Life* (1913), as well as poetry focusing on Christ and descriptions of the Castilian landscape, where he sought out the hidden soul of the people. Although he moved from pro-European positions to a mystical vision of Spain opposed to rationalism and scientific enquiry, when rector of Salamanca University he clashed with the fascist General Millán Astray, was sacked and died shortly afterwards.

Juan de Valdés Leal (1622–1690): Painter, sculptor and architect from Seville who was commissioned by the city's archbishop to paint a series of scenes from the life of Saint Ambrose. These were taken by Marshal Soult, who in 1810 converted the archiepiscopal palace into his barracks during the Napoleonic invasion of the Peninsula. Lorca refers to one of Valdés Leal's paintings depicting the horrors of death and the decay of the flesh.

The Valladolid Museum of Fine Arts: Lorca saw this collection, which was opened in 1842 with artefacts from monasteries dissolved by the liberal reformer Mendizábal, in 1917, on the same trip to Castile during which he visited Burgos, Ávila and Santo Domingo de Silos. The sculptures he mentions are now in the collection of the National Museum of Sculpture in Valladolid.

Dr Francisco Vallés (1524–1592): Born in Covarrubias, he lived most of his life in Alcalá de Henares, where was Professor of Medicine from 1555 to 1572, when he was appointed to doctor to Philip II. He was given the nickname of 'The Divine' when he cured the king of his gout. Famed for his interest in dissecting corpses, he once told the inhabitants of Covarrubias to pull down the town walls and let in some fresh air as the best way to end a typhoid epidemic.

Jan Weenix (1642–1719): A prolific Dutch painter who preferred dead game and hunting subjects, which he beautified as in 'The White Peacock' and numerous paintings of dead rabbits, hares and swans.

Ignacio Zuloaga (1870–1945): Basque artist who for many years lived between Paris and Segovia. He painted landscapes of a noble but impoverished Castile – his 'black Spain' – as well as portraits of diligent peasants and writers such as Miguel de Unamuno and Ramón del Valle-Inclán.

PUBLISHER'S ACKNOWLEDGEMENTS

❖ ❖ ❖ ❖ ❖

We would like to thank Juan Blas Abando, Fidel López Álvarez, Michael Bollen, Lourdes Gómez, Fanchita González Batlle, Iñigo Gurruchaga, Vicky Hayward, Hamish Irwin, Will Irwin, Sara Maté-Fernández and Christopher Moriarty, all of whom gave much appreciated advice and assistance.

Justus Oehler in Berlin and Sue Lamble in London have – as always – produced notably handsome designs for the cover and the text, while Julian Bell's illustrations are more than worthy of this, the first British edition of Federico García Lorca's first book.

THE FACE OF SPAIN
Gerald Brenan

Afterword by Michael Jacobs

Gerald Brenan returned to Spain in 1949 for the first time since the Civil War. He was determined to see what had become of the country he loved, to speak to ordinary people and to experience life in small towns unvisited by foreigners. He had earlier lived in a remote village in the Sierra Nevada – now he returned to a land in the grip of famine where *guerrilleros* roamed the mountains and thousands of people were reduced to living in caves.

Whether searching for his friend Lorca's unmarked grave, musing on the history of the great mosque in Córdoba and old synagogues in Toledo or chatting to provincial shopkeepers, Brenan was unfailingly perceptive. Despite being shadowed by police informers and harangued by Francoist priests, he was undeterred, and this witty and humane account of his visit illuminates a chapter of Spanish history that remains almost unknown. Franco's regime has now vanished, but its ghosts continue to haunt Spain. When they were still alive, no one described the ogres and their victims more vividly than Gerald Brenan.

'Fascinating' *New Statesman*

'The ideal travel book … miraculous' *The Observer*

'A brilliant interpreter of Spain to the rest of the world'
The Times

'Britain's greatest Hispanist travels through Franco's bleak Spain. His account is unforgettable.' Ian Gibson

paperback

also available

THE SLAVES OF THE COOL MOUNTAINS

Alan Winnington

Beijing 1956: foreign correspondent Alan Winnington heard reports of slaves being freed in the mountains of south-west China. The following year he travelled to Yunnan province and spent several months with the head-hunting Wa and the slave-owing Norsu and Jingpaw. From that journey *The Slaves of the Cool Mountains*, hailed by Neal Ascherson as 'one of the classics of modern English travel writing', was born.

The first European to enter and leave these areas alive, Winnington met a slave-owner who assessed his value at five silver ingots ('Your age is against you, but as a curiosity you would fetch a decent price'), a head-hunter who a fortnight earlier had killed a man in order to improve his own rice harvest and a sorcerer struggling against the modern medicines sapping his authority and livelihood. Meeting recently released slaves was a scoop of which most journalists can only dream – 'Nobody will ever see them again be able to see them as I saw them' – and Winnington's account of their struggle to come to terms with new-found freedom is unforgettable.

'A clear, striking account' *Time Out*

'A fascinating study of a little known pocket of humanity'
The Age (Melbourne)

'One of Britain's greatest foreign correspondents – curious, witty and adventurous' Jonathan Mirsky, *The Observer*

paperback

NINETY-TWO DAYS
Travels in Guiana and Brazil

Evelyn Waugh

Afterword by Pauline Melville

In 1932 Evelyn Waugh abandoned the salons of Mayfair for the savannah and rainforest of what was then British Guiana, and, although even his comic imagination could not have invented the characters he met in South America, only he could have described them so perfectly. A cattle-rancher who claimed to be a close friend of the Virgin Mary, a missionary with a pet toad that ate burning cigarette-ends, a gold-prospector who believed he was guided through the jungle by speaking parrots, and numerous others live on in Waugh's mordant prose, as do his vivid descriptions of Guyana's landscapes. The author's journey – on foot, horseback and by boat – was extremely arduous, but he remained an unfailingly astute observer, offering a fascinating picture of the Amerindian peoples through whose lands he travelled.

In the Afterword, award-winning novelist Pauline Melville explores the connections between Waugh's experiences in the region of Guyana from which her own family hails and *A Handful of Dust*, one of Waugh's greatest novels, giving a fascinating insight into both the creative process and the mind of the man himself.

'A comic genius' *Times Literary Supplement*

'Exquisitely miserable' Nicholas Lezard, *The Guardian*

'He will be admired as long as there are people who can read'
Daily Telegraph

paperback

THE ARAN ISLANDS
J.M. Synge

Illustrations by Jack B. Yeats

'Go to the Aran Islands. Live there as if you were one of the people themselves; express a life that has never found expression.' J.M. Synge did exactly as his friend W.B. Yeats suggested and, revisiting these harsh yet beautiful specks of land off the west coast of Ireland over a period of four years, created a literary masterpiece.

Synge immersed himself in the islanders' lives as they steered their curraghs through Atlantic waves, mourned their dead, celebrated weddings and suffered the horrors of eviction. *The Aran Islands* weaves their stories with Synge's own, and the result, as Colm Tóibín has remarked is that, 'Unlike most travel books of 100 years ago, it has not dated at all.'

Serif's is the first paperback edition in which Jack B. Yeats's remarkable drawings, commissioned for the 1911 Dublin edition, have appeared alongside Synge's haunting prose, making this classic work available once again in the form its author intended.

'This is travel writing of a special kind' *Irish Independent*

'Captivating ... profoundly attuned to the spirit of the place'
Times Literary Supplement

'Travel writing of the highest order' *Time Out*

paperback

TRAVELS IN WICKLOW, WEST KERRY AND CONNEMARA
J.M. Synge

Illustrations by Jack B. Yeats

J.M. Synge was a tireless traveller who, while celebrating the beauties of the Irish landscape, never flinched from describing the harsh, unromantic reality of rural life. Jack B. Yeats's evocative drawings were intended to accompany these accounts of Synge's travels and they are now published together again for the first time in 100 years.

Capturing the embers of a dying culture, the great playwright walks, drinks and talks with a rich assortment of country people, offering unforgettable descriptions of the Puck Fair at Killorglin and horse-racing on the strand near Dingle, of remote cottages and isolated fishing villages.

Seamus Heaney wrote of Synge in 'Glanmore Eclogue' that he

Was never happier than when he was on the road
With people on their uppers. Loneliness
Was his passport through the world. Midge-angels
On the face of the water, the first drop before thunder ...
His spirit lives for me in things like that.

Synge's wandering spirit, as well as the farmers and tinkers, weavers and boat builders he befriended, live on in these pages, which cannot fail to delight anyone who loves Ireland and her literature.

'Admirable' Seamus Heaney

'Synge's travel writings are particularly fascinating' *The Irish Times*

paperback

'I do not think altogether the worse of a book for having survived the author a generation or two.'

William Hazlitt